AN
INSPIRED
Life

10 stories to inspire you to design a life you will love.

Curated by The Corporate Escapists
www.thecorporateescapists.com

An Inspired Life

All Rights Reserved

No part of this book may be reproduced or transmitted in any form or by any means, electronic or mechanical, including photocopying, recording or any information story and retrieval system, without permission in writing from the curator The Corporate Escapists

Are you living an inspired life?

It is not a question a lot of us get asked nor do we know how to answer.

So let me ask you this "Are you following your passion?" You know that dream you had when you were younger and wanted to pursue.

If you said no, then this is the book for you.

After years of following the corporate pathway, everything in my life started to crash including my health, my finances, my relationships, even my own identity.

The past 6 years have been a journey of healing and learning. Healing from my past and also learning that all of the life events that had taken place have led me to this moment.

The moment where I can wake up each day inspired, feeling loved, actually wanting to get out of bed to start the day, working with people I adore, and most of all, having a sense of purpose.

Learning to live an inspired life takes courage. Courage to dream again and courage to follow your dreams.

This book is filled with 10 beautiful, inspirational, and courageous stories and tips from real women who are all living an inspired life.

They are all showing you what is possible and how you can learn from them to live AN INSPIRED LIFE.

AN INSPIRED *Life*

Table of contents

MY STORY..1
   Christine Innes

COURAGE TO SAY NO...12
   Kleo Merrick

HAVE YOU GOT THE GUTS..21
   Justine Lawson

STRUGGLE, STRENGTH, SURVIVAL, SHINE.......................29
   Ana Angelique

FINDING THE GIRL IN THE YELLOW TUTU.......................41
   Kylie James

THE SPIRITUAL JOURNEY AND EVOLUTION OF THE SOUL.....51
   Lisa Ohtaras

ASPIRE TO INSPIRE..62
   Terri Tonkin

BROKEN TO BE BRILLIANT..72
   Carolyn Maree Fernando

SURVIVIAL MODE..80
   Kristin Sullivan

YOUR STORY IS NOT OVER...91
   Tamara Hall

Christine Innes

CEO AND FOUDER OF THE CORPORATE ESCAPISTS
EDITOR IN CHIEF OF THE CORPORATE ESCAPISTS MAGAZINE
INTERNATIONAL BEST SELLING AUTHOR

Your time to shine

Dedication

"Turn your wounds into wisdom" - Oprah

It's 6 am and I am already running late. I quickly get dressed for work: putting on the designer suit, the heels, the makeup, and the jewellery. This is my suit of armour to get me through the day.

If you had asked me 6 years ago if I was happy, I would of course have said yes. However, at the same time, I knew deep down inside that something was missing. Something that I just couldn't put my finger on. I knew where I was heading. Well actually, it was that I was doing what was expected of me. You know the drill. Go to school, get a good education, get a job, get married, have kids, work your way up the corporate ladder, and then when you retire, that is when you can enjoy life.

So what was I worried about? I had it all figured out. Or so I thought!

In 2015 my life changed. I was working in the corporate world, working my way up that golden corporate ladder when everything started to crumble. It began when I was diagnosed with two life-changing illnesses. This was only the start of how my life changed completely in just one year.

I left my corporate career in what I now call my not-so-gracious exit. I also left my toxic and unfixable marriage filed for bankruptcy and ended up having to sleep on my parents' couch. Quite the change from a corporate career to being broke and broken - both physically and financially.

You can say that year changed my life. My story could have stopped there. Unable to see any light at the end of the tunnel, I thought, "This is it.". I guess it wouldn't be much of a story if it stopped there.

During the next few years, I needed to regroup and find out who I was. During this time I realised that one of the key areas in my life was my career. But who was I without it?

Who was Christine?
What did she want from life?
What were her goals?
What are her dreams?

All of these questions I had never asked myself before.

It was like I had found a new lease on life, and I needed to discover who I really was.

The flame has been lit:

"Anything you can imagine you can create" - Oprah

With the first whiff of fresh air, I knew that there was something brewing inside of me. That something was to find ME. The real me. The one without the suit of armour shielding myself from that world.

So, how does one change their life? How can you set a new destination without even knowing where you are going? It would be like hopping in the car, putting it into drive and just hitting the highway with no map, no directions and no plan.

This was how I felt.. I knew that I needed to be the one in the driver's seat and also have some idea of where I wanted to go.

This is how my journey of self-discovery started.

Trying to figure out my next destination, I recalled a few years ago when a friend of mine was talking about a concept called "An Ideal Day". Nothing like groundhog day. It is a day that you can have on repeat, a day that inspires you to be the best version of yourself. A day where you are surrounded by people you love, where you are inspired to follow your dreams and passion.

This immediately sparked something inside of me. I found a quiet space and dove deep within myself to create my own Ideal Day.

As I closed my eyes and connected to my heart, my own feelings and desires, I gave myself the permission to be in the creative moment. I started with how I wanted to feel when I woke up in the morning. I put all my feelings into the process and wanted to ensure I felt all the emotions. As I leaned into the process more, I could begin to feel the touch of the sheets as I stretched out in the morning, lying in my own bed, with rays of sunlight beaming through my window. A far cry from sleeping on my parents' couch!

I delved further into the visualisation, and could start to see how the rest of the day would unfold.

The people I wanted to spend time with, the environment I would be in, the types of moments I wanted to experience. The big moment came when I could see myself sharing my story to help inspire others. It was the first time that I felt the flame had been lit and I could start to see the future I wanted, and I was actually allowing myself to dream again.

What I know now is this is part of the Law of Attraction, and as I continued on my own self-discovery journey I learned more about it and the power of my own thoughts. If you have not yet discovered the Law of Attraction, it is the ability to attract what we focus on into our lives. It is a game-changer. I use it every day and love sharing it with others.

Living again

"If you want your life to be more rewarding , you have to change the way you think" - Oprah

Over the next few years, I continued to focus on my self-discovery and healing. Every day I became stronger and also gained more clarity into the life I wanted. I knew I was ready to chase after it.

What I had been learning in my journey -especially about the thoughts I was projecting out- was part of creating my new life.

I knew that just the visualisation was not going to be enough. I needed to take ownership of where my life was heading and take action. It was the action that was the key component. The key to unlocking all my potential and desires.

To start with changing my thoughts, I needed to change the words I was speaking. The next big part of creating my ideal life was to let go of who I was and focus on the woman I was becoming. One word that kept coming up was "perfection". I had always tried to be perfect for everyone and please them all: I was a perfectionist and a people pleaser.

I kept asking myself, what is "perfection" anyway?

I had the realisation that perfection never really exists. Perfection is something that you are always striving for and is simply unattainable. Each time I reached a point I thought I would be happy with, I would always find something else that needed to be fixed.

I can remember my corporate days vividly, sitting there with several emails in draft as I wanted them to be perfect. To make sure the grammar, the tone, the message were all perfect. I think now how much time I wasted and how unproductive I actually was in trying to achieve perfection.

It made me realise that I needed to be happy where I was in life. The "right now" is exactly where I needed to be, however, it doesn't mean that I am going to stay here. I also needed to learn to enjoy the journey. Enjoy every moment: the good, the bad and the not so good.

It certainly was a strange concept, especially as I love planning and love being organised. I would always have my to-do list handy and tick off each task. Yet one of the key parts of the Law of Attraction is to have fun. Yet how can you have fun when you feel lost without a plan or even when you feel like you have so much to achieve?

What I realised is that this whole journey was not about me creating the life I wanted, it was also allowing me to choose myself. To have the courage to make mistakes and to be human.
I was on the right track and I needed to keep going and keep learning how to live away and share this with others.

As I moved forward, people started to notice the change in me. They noticed the spark, the fire inside and they wanted to know the secret. I now share with my clients a quote I have created. It brings together all of the learnings so far, to help you create your own reality

The Three Key Principles in Life

As I started to share my story with others, I realised that I had based this on three principles.
These principles changed my life.

DREAMS + ACTION = REALITY

The three key principles I have created are:

1. Dream - Create your own ideal day.
2. Values - Find out what you stand for, because if you stand for nothing you will fall for everything.
3. Your future self - Look forward to your own future self. Only glance back to see how far you have come.

Dream you say, but all I can see right now is the life I am not happy with. This is the key. We all have dreams and then most of us forget them and we go down the rabbit hole of following the life that is expected of us. You know the drill. We go to school, get the grades, go to university or start working, and when we retire that is when we will have some fun.

Well, I am calling BS on this.. YEP Bull Shit.. Why can we not have the life we want. Why do we have to wait until retirement to have fun?

The first of these key principles is permitting yourself to dream again and to create your own ideal day. A day you will love and can not wait to do over again.

Let's talk values. Your core values are your foundation for life. They are what grounds you, they show who you are as a person and what you stand for.

Values are something you should be proud of, willing to scream them from the rooftops proudly. I spent a lot of time working on my own values and integrating them into my life.

To give you a glimpse, here are my own top 10 values:

1. Love - Even when I feel the fear and the self-doubt creeps in I lean into love, especially leaning into loving myself even more. To this day I am still learning this and learning to love my flaws as well. This is not about ego, it is showing kindness to yourself and also allowing yourself to see the beauty in yourself and others.
2. Trust - Learning to trust myself, my decisions and others. It is also about trusting the process, which is a major part of the Law of Attraction. The universe has your back.
3. Faith - Having the faith within myself that I can achieve my goals.
4. Authenticity - Always be ME! No more pretending and hiding behind a suit of armour. Simply be me, I am enough.
5. Family - Family comes first.
6. Integrity - always show up every day as my true self and be consistent in my thoughts and behaviours.
7. Fun - Have more and more fun every day. The more fun I have the more success I have in my life and my business.
8. Dream - Don't stop dreaming. I allow myself to be creative and bring on those big dreams and goals for myself.
9. Loyalty - Be loyal to myself and others.
10. Freedom - Give myself permission to be the person I choose to be and without judgement towards myself and others.

Your future self is a way of looking at the person you want to become and starting to embody them. It is a way for you to stop looking back in the past and dwelling on everything that has not worked til now and look towards your bright future.

Creating your life

Imagine for a moment you could honestly say that you had a life that was filled with love, joy, abundance and happiness. How would that make you feel? How tall would you be standing?
How proud would you be?

I can honestly say that I have all of this in my life and I feel amazing and blessed. I walk with my head held high and I feel so proud of myself that I have created this. I am surrounded by loving, beautiful and inspiring people, I am lit up and I am creating my own happiness and opportunities that bring me joy. None of this would have been possible without having made the decision to change life and to give myself the permission to change.

I can admit that for most of my life I sat in what I call the "victim mindset". You know, the "poor me", "feel sorry for me", "help me - yet do it for me". When everything in my life was crumbling I am pretty sure I said all those and much more.

I was having a pity party for myself. You know those parties where you sit and feel sorry for yourself, eat junk food, cry and can't see the light at the end of the tunnel.

When I stopped having the victim mindset I started to see things as learning lessons, and not just that it was happening to me, it was happening for me.

Let me say that again.

It was not happening **to** me, it was happening **for** me.

This powerful sentence can change the way you view all obstacles you face. It gives you a different perspective and shifts you into a more positive mindset.

Now I see the difficult times in my life as a blessing. These challenges have made me into the person I am today and has given me the opportunity to create the life I have. I would not change any of it. When you are standing at a crossroad in your life, you are always given an opportunity. These choices give you the opportunity to either see the decision as an obstacle or as a lesson in life.

For me, I will always choose the lesson and see it as something I need to learn from and it allows me to continue to grow as a person.

Let the magic begin

Knowing what I know now, I can recognise the signs from the universe that my life was crumbling, but I was not ready to listen. Now learning to appreciate all the moments gives me the ability to recognise just how blessed I am.

Never underestimate your own power!

Everyone has the magic inside of them, and following my Three Key Principles will give you the insight into the life you want to create, a life where you can be back in the driver's seat and set the destination of your own choice.

The Key

Over the past 6 years, I have gone from being broke and broken, to having a life where I am filled with passion and joy and able to inspire and empower others.

I know that if I can do it, you can too.

The key to remember is to have fun, have trust and faith within yourself and remember: you are worthy enough to achieve your goals.

With this you can achieve anything.

Love and light,

x Christine

Power Summary

Let's do a quick recap of the Three Key Principles:

1. Dream - Create your own ideal day.
2. Values - Find out what you stand for, because if you stand for anything you will fall for everything.
3. Your future self - Look forward to your own future self. Only glance back to see how far you have come.

Success Actions

Here are Three Success Actions that you can do right now to make a big impact in your life.

1. Give yourself permission to have FUN!
2. Give yourself permission to DREAM!
3. Give yourself permission to BE YOU!

Courage to say no

To all those inspired and daring, live your life on your terms!

"When you can truly say no, you can embrace the yes"
Kleo Merrick

Where did I go? Who is this person I see standing before me?

Yes, I recognise her as being me, while looking at her reflection in the mirror. But when did I become so incredibly disconnected with her, who she truly is, what she stands for, what she believes?

What happened to that spark, that incredible fire, and drive?

Is it gone?

When did I lose myself?

I remember running an 'Online Courses for Entrepreneurs' workshop at the very beginning of 2020. It was a great presentation, was always well received by the attendees and never failed to have what I call 'extreme a-ha moments' for the entire audience.

And yet, even though my presentation had been practiced repeatedly, perfected to the point of a sales prediction of 20-30% conversion, this time it was different. There was something missing – it felt empty.

In a blink of an eye, I saw myself jump out of my body and suddenly the whole presentation went into super slow-motion. It felt like Dr Strange being pushed out of his body by the Ancient One, just like in the movie, and I was literally standing beside myself.

After doing the typical 'hand wave in front of my face', like you also see in the movies; I looked around the room and took stock of where I was.

I was upstairs from the pub in a dark, dank, and musty smelling room, which was the only one I could afford to hire. The kind of place where you had to check all the supposed clean glassware for lipstick marks. I know this is sounding picky but, I'm ex-hospitality and can spot a chipped or dirty glass from a mile away, you get the idea.

Surrounded by people that I didn't know, didn't particularly like and didn't particularly want to work with in the future. They certainly didn't care to know me and only wanted me for my skills and knowledge, which they probably wouldn't listen to and then blame me for it not working for them. My prospects for getting any new quality clients weren't looking good.

...And there it is.

After jumping back into my body, I seamlessly continued with the presentation, but this time my unconscious and muscle memory took over and continued, kind of like when you're driving on autopilot, but your mind is deeply processing. Whilst I questioned what the f**k just happened?

I felt vacant, lost, and empty and my wicked sense of humour and that cheeky twinkle in my eye, were nowhere to be seen.

This set into motion and started a path of self-questioning to identify who I was and more importantly why I was:

When had I ever allowed myself and my clients to come into this crappy environment?

Why had I attracted this kind of client, that I couldn't even connect with on any level?

What was I even doing here?

What happened?

Teaching my audience about online business, surely there was a better way to do this?

Was I even happy? Who was I?

I felt like I'd bottomed out. In short, I'd lost my identity.

You see, the way I grew up there was never any praise or celebration of my achievements. In fact, there was never any focus on my anything, because my parents and even grandparents were so incredibly consumed with our families' business that anything else even remotely significant in my life, very much fell by the wayside.

With an overbearing, overcritical mother with ridiculously high expectations of me as a child and even throughout adulthood, nothing I did would ever be good enough. Forced to grow up from a very young age and take responsibility, not only for myself, but my two younger sisters, and to some degree my older brother, much to his disgust. This eradicated me from ever having a normal, playful, and carefree childhood.

My father on the other hand was extremely one-dimensional and easy-going, but who's wrath, absenteeism, and sarcasm had the ability to cut you to the core. Again, I knew that I would never be good enough for the approval of my father and just like I had done with my mother, I used this to drive me forward and strive to be better, every day.

I learned very quickly to be a 'good girl', do as I was told, always tell the truth, always think of others before thinking of yourself, and never upset the apple cart. And when my siblings made a mistake or put a foot wrong, I took this as my own failing, as it was my responsibility.

Even though I was yelled at and screamed at countless times, for things that I didn't do, I still took it. But it was the 'stonewalling' – the ignoring for punishment that killed my soul.

And yet, instead of allowing this to crush me, I used this as armour, hardness, directness, and drive. I strived and pushed myself more and more to do better, with the hope that one day, it would be good enough.

But it always came at a price, throughout my childhood I carried a sadness and an anger towards my parents for never being aware of the pain that I was in and their failure to recognise what they'd created. And the regret of never having been free to express myself or have my opinion valued.

So, whilst running the workshop with my Dr. Strange moment, I began to question my life, not just my business, not just my childhood... but everything!

And realised I was running away from pain and emptiness.

This was because everything that I'd ever done in my life was desperately trying to please others and avoid the pain of disappointing them.

Which meant I was going around in circles running away from the monsters I, in fact, had **created for myself.**

Don't get me wrong it wasn't all bad, I'm happily married, a great mama to my munchkin and step-mama. And I've had quite a few achievements in my life: successful business owner and entrepreneur, author of 3 books (4 including this one), returning to study and doing my Masters, and many others.

But the empty feeling that I identified during the workshop was also present after each one of those achievements and left them dulled.

Then one day, during yet another completely nonsensical argument, suddenly, I was done! Finished, ka-put! I said NO!

Now I don't mean just a little 'no', I mean a HECK FREAKIN' NOOOOOOOOOOOOOOO!

A 'NO' that Maria Von Trapp really wanted to shout from the top of that hill in 'The Sound of Music', because her life was at such an incredible impasse, but she wouldn't dare. You get it, it was insanely powerful and symbolic... and shockingly elating.

It felt like my life was a knitted jumper that belonged to someone else, it never fit properly, with a loose thread that I just dared to pull and the whole thing unravelled before my eyes and disappeared into oblivion.

From this I began to recognise so much of my life that I'd been holding back, limiting, and of course, judging myself. Stifling my progress, constantly fighting against myself, and blindly battling everything and everyone in my path. I felt as if I'd broken up with the worst relationship I'd ever had in my life and after 43 years I was free. And calm, with incredible clarity and resolve.

So, I'd lost my identity and... gained my freedom?

It's funny because sometimes we get so attached to things and hang on for dear life because we're so petrified of losing them. Not realising or focusing on what we could gain once we surrender and let go.

I dove into my life coaching resources to gain some understanding and more importantly, language to be able to process this change. And with the help of my good friend Cathy (a Creatrix Transformologist), I began to release past pains and navigate my new world. And started to slowly stitch together my new jumper, with my colours, my threads, my pattern, my design and for my life moving forward.

One of the golden nuggets that impacted me during this process was an awareness of how I was driven and where my motivation for life came from. I wanted to share this with you, in the hope that it imparts some wisdom, as for me this explained it to a tea. The principle that explains all human behaviour – the Pain and Pleasure Principle.

You see, as humans we are motivated by either running away from pain or running towards pleasure:

1. Moving Away from Pain:

We will do anything we must to move away from the pain in our lives. For example: simple things like, 'I don't want to cook tonight', cause us pain, because we can't be bothered, we must decide what groceries are needed, etc. So, it's easier to contend with, 'Let's get takeaway!' This quickly removes the pain from the situation, no one complains, everyone is happy. This solves the problem by moving away from pain.

The other example is of that in my behaviour above, I never wanted to get in trouble and desperately needed approval and would do anything to move away from that type of pain. So inadvertently my actions were driven by moving away from pain. This behaviour is done by most people simply because they don't know any other way. This is not exactly something we are taught at school.

Unfortunately, this is very unresourceful and not sustainable, meaning it would be very difficult to continue motivating yourself using this strategy long-term. In short, over time something would always have to give.

2. Moving towards Pleasure:

This is the flip side, where the actions you take are driven by the pleasure and rewards to be received. An example of this is when you're wanting to lose weight, and you're motivated by how you will feel once you've achieved your goal weight. How those new clothes will fit on you and for all the lovely comments you'll receive from people.

This behaviour is much more resourceful and sustainable, meaning it's very easy to continue behaving this way, long term.

How do you know if you're in a similar situation or impasse? Ask yourself:

- Have you done a heap of personal development, but there's still something hidden and just out of reach?
- Are you pushing yourself too hard and constantly disappointed with the results you get?
- Do you feel like you're running a marathon but there's never any finish line?

Be honest with your answers, or you can try to journal to discover your truth.

Once I realised that I was moving away from the pain in my life, this all came to a head and just like that, I was out of my storm. This awareness enabled me to stop this behaviour and change the way I motivate myself and of course the ripple effects that this creates for those around me. It's enabled me to now create the life that I wish to live on my terms.

And yet because I had the courage to say 'No' and everything encapsulated within this, it now presupposes that I also have the power to say 'Yes'! To welcome glory to my life, which is by far the most powerful aspect of all of this!

I like to look at it like this; would you prefer to run away from monsters all your life? It would be exhausting! Or you can choose to chase rainbows, which would be exhilarating.

What will you choose?

> *"Dare to chase your dreams"*
> Kleo Merrick

Love your journey

Kleo Merrick xxx

Have you got the guts?

To the little Justine who has always had my back and been that voice. I hear you and thank you ♥

"Do the best you can until you know better, then when you know better, do better" - Maya Angelou

I moved to Australia in 1998 as my family had migrated to Brisbane three years prior from New Zealand. I had not lived in the same city as my family, since I was 13, due to attending boarding school and then university. I felt that they didn't fully know who I was and I wanted them to get to know me.

I had been in Brisbane for about four years and was working in the city earning $37,000. I'd recently asked for a pay rise and went from $32K to $37K, a massive windfall in my opinion. For a while I was quite happy. I had a job where I was somewhat valued, I had met the guy I wanted to marry and he got on well with my family. #WINNING. But then I had a thought, "Is this it? Was this job going to get me where I wanted to go?". If someone had asked me at the time, "where do you want to go?", I would have just shrugged my shoulders and said, "I have no idea". What I had was all I knew, wasn't it? This is where the journey to me started.

Growing up for me involved being compliant, being a good girl. If I didn't do as I was told there was hell to pay. If I ever thought it was a good idea to go against my Dad and his authority, I suffered the consequences.

My Dad and I had a complex yet simple relationship. He wasn't my birth father, but was my Dad in every other sense of the word. It was complex as the parent / child relationships can be but at the same time, simple, as Dad was the head of the house and if you stepped out of line, well, you get the picture. To reduce the risk of me being yelled at, I would spend most of my time in my bedroom.

Where I could, I would arrange to spend time at a friend's house because there I would definitely be safe. When I think back on my childhood, I can recall good times and happy moments. For all intents and purposes, it was a stereotypical happy childhood, but it left me with some scars.

Note: parents parent the best way they know how, with the knowledge that they have. This means that they parent as a reaction (good or bad) to their experiences.

My scars.....

- Do as you're told and you stay safe
- If you ever become a parent, you'll probably do a shit job
- You are not loveable
- Men are in charge
- Be on guard always
- Authority figures are to be obeyed

When I finally arrived at boarding school at the age of thirteen, all I felt was relief. I didn't know what to expect, but I didn't care. What I came to understand in my five years there, was that it was totally okay to be me. I felt freedom for the first time in a long time.

Throughout my teenage years, I began to learn how to trust myself. My Dad still had influence over some of the decisions that I made, so this process was a slow one. My inner compass (I often refer to this as my intuition / gut feeling) became stronger as I got older and it felt good. Once I left school and started university, my personal growth journey started in earnest. My first year felt like being in a tumble dryer and I experienced a plethora of emotions. It was also the year that I finally told my Dad that I wasn't going to listen to his advice regarding my education. He pretty much told me that I was on my own.

Whilst I felt proud for listening to my gut, I also agonised over my decision as it meant that I didn't have the support of someone I thought would always support me. I finished my degree and scored a job in a place that was a good fit for me. It was a great experience for my first full-time job and it complimented my degree.

Fast-forward a couple of years and I'm in another country, in a dead end job asking "is this it?". With my previous knowledge and experience, it was time to listen to my gut.

So that's what I did.

Deciding to listen to my gut feeling was the easy part. I knew that whatever came next was going to challenge the status quo. And I wondered if I was up for it. I had an inkling that further study was most likely in my future. And I remember vowing that if I ever went back to university, it would be too soon.

I worried about failing and investing money that didn't yield a result. I never really felt very smart whilst completing my degree and I wondered if I was intelligent enough to do another degree or even still, complete a postgraduate qualification. At the time, no-one in my immediate family had completed university except my Dad. So I just didn't know if I had the pedigree to level up.

I thought about taking the easy route and staying where I was, by being grateful for what I had. No one was pushing me to do better. And then there was the money. How was I going to afford the study? How was I going to support myself? If I managed to find a part-time job that could fit around the study, would I actually make enough to survive? There was also a high likelihood that I wouldn't be able to receive support from the government, so it really was up to me. I asked myself how badly I wanted to get out of my current situation and create better opportunities for myself. Even as I write this now, I think, wow, that was a lot to overcome.

And you want to know the best bit? I did overcome all of those thoughts, fears, and worries. I invested in consulting with a Careers Counsellor who helped me decide on a course (it was a postgraduate qualification), and completed it within the specified time frame. This decision to level up provided me the opportunity to grow and make a difference in people's lives. And you know what else? Those thoughts and fears I had, were nothing compared to what happened after I made the decision....

I was forced to leave my job a week earlier than planned because my employer wasn't happy about me leaving and my boyfriend (now my husband) was made redundant -effective immediately- the Friday prior to me starting my study. He had agreed to support me whilst I completed my study and to add insult to injury, we had only just moved into a new rental property where the rent was about $60 more per week.

> I could have let all that dismantle my plans, but I didn't.

> I could have thought, ":we won't survive financially so I better get a full time job and forget about the study", but I didn't.

> I could have thought, "this is all too hard, I just want to go back to easy and comfortable", but I didn't.

This experience helped me to understand that I'm worth the effort and that I can get through hardship. Even better than that, I can go through hard things and become a better person because of them. I believe that not having things come easy will test your resolve and if you continue to strive for something, eventually you'll get there. As I reflect on the experience, I can see that my self confidence and trust in myself grew.

As a woman, I find we are sent so many messages in society that we perceive ourselves to not be enough or worthy. Through experience I saw that I have control over how I perceive myself and that is so important for every woman to know. I have control over my narrative so why not make it a helpful positive one.

As I now tell my clients, no one can make you feel anything, you do that to yourself. I learned that I'm worth investing in and as Marie Forleo says, everything is figureoutable.

When I remember the thought I had all those years ago, "Is this it?", I recall feeling stuck, because right in that moment, the last thing I wanted to do was entertain the idea of having to complete further study. To enable me to move from that stuck feeling, I imagined what my life might be like if I allowed everything to stay as it was. I felt pain, resignation, a heaviness that threatened to never go away. I asked myself if I could live with this and imagined myself as someone who was unhappy and alone. This was not the picture I wanted to have as my future self.

Since returning to university and obtaining my Graduate Diploma, I have provided services to many clients here in Australia and in New Zealand. I have created a career in an industry that I care a lot about, and have grown in confidence year after year. I have continued to invest in myself and my education as I am a work in progress. I know this is how things will be for the foreseeable future and I'm so okay with this.

Note: I have recently informed my husband that he needs to think of my constant yearning to learn and improve as a hobby. I let him know that it is highly likely that this will be a mainstay in my life, or our life for quite some time.

Up until recently, I had been working as an employee in the same industry I started in about 16 years ago, and thoroughly enjoy empowering my clients to believe in themselves. Since becoming a parent, I have been working on my small business. It is certainly not where I want it to be but if the past 20 years have taught me anything, it's to be patient and have faith in the timing. I feel I'm well equipped to stay the course. I know my husband scratches his head sometimes wondering why I don't just keep it simple and ditch the small business. Since I made the hobby comment, he has been slightly more understanding as to why I stick with it.

Currently, I work with clients one-on-one and love group facilitation. I'm constantly creating content for my social media channels and have become comfortable with being in front of the camera. I work hard at being a Mum and a wife and strive to have a marriage that thrives on open communication. I also make sure that I carve out time for me so that I have an opportunity to fill my cup. By doing this I'm able to give more and be present more.

My goal has always been to empower and and I have so much information in my head that I am busting to get out into the world. The clients in my industry have been the lucky recipients of my knowledge and care for over 15 years and now it's time for everyone else to experience what I have to offer!

> "Your time is limited, so don't waste it living someone else's life. Don't be trapped by Dogma - which is living with the results of other people's thinking. Don't let the noise of others' opinions drown out your own inner voice. And most important, have the courage to follow your heart and intuition"
>
> Steve Jobs

Lastly, here are some words of wisdom I'd like to leave with you.

- If that voice inside keeps piping up with a consistent message, it may just be time to listen

- Post-it notes are part of my success strategy. I stick them to boards I have around my office so that I can record and reflect on all my ideas.

- Get clear on what you want, and watch your decision-making get easier.

- If you think it, it can happen.

- When it all seems too hard, that's the time you must dig in and keep going.

- Have people around that support and challenge you. Don't assume these people are your family either. Often your family want to protect you and not have you out there risking it all.

- Know your worth.

- Ask for help.

Struggle, Strength, Survival, Shine

To my three gorgeous children: Thank you for your unconditional love, support and friendship, especially during those really tough times. I admire your resilience, strength, dedication, and positivity; You inspire me daily. Thank you for always believing in me and being my biggest fans. Keep shining and just being wonderfully you. I love you.

"If I had the strength to endure everything that I did go through, then I have the strength to keep moving forward and to make things better." Ana Angelique

Part 1: Who Is She?

I grew up hating the colour of my skin. I grew up being embarrassed that I didn't have Australian parents, like everyone else seemed to have. What I felt like on the inside, never matched the person who looked back at me in the mirror every day. I wanted to be taller and whiter, with emerald green eyes and dark wavy hair. I didn't want such a mixed heritage. I didn't want to be an only child. I didn't want to be a girl. I just wanted to fit in.

But I also wanted to be remembered.

I wanted to make changes – massive, global changes. I wanted to make the world a better place to live in, because even as a little girl, I saw so much that shouldn't be and so much of what could be. I wanted to live a life of travel and luxury, surrounded by pretty things. I wanted to push past the ordinary and the mundane. I wanted to make such a huge impact that I'd be known by name alone, and I'd be respected and somewhat feared because everyone would know that I was someone who shouldn't be toyed with. I wanted to be taken seriously.

But every time I tried, I was told and shown that I couldn't.

I was laughed at when I told everyone that I wanted to be a powerful female leader when I grew up: that I wanted to run a country to make it better, or own a business that was so successful and global that it was a household name. Not possible, they said. I was reminded that I was only a girl and that things would be different if I was a boy. I was told that I was dreaming and that I didn't know how the world worked. I was shown how things were always done and how difficult it was to do anything different. I was made to conform and adhere to the rules that others made and maintained, and I was punished if I tried to do it differently... at home, at school, at work, and in my personal relationships.

But every now and then, I got a glimpse of what could be.

And so I pushed on.

Part 2: Childhood Games and Imposed Rules

I grew up in suburbia. Outer suburbia. Out enough to recall having a few empty blocks of land on our street where horses grazed for years, before they were moved out to be replaced with brick houses. The streets were wide and the cars few.

I was the youngest on my half of the street, the youngest among my godparents' children and any of the children of family friends. All my relatives lived overseas, so it was just me and my parents.

Mum was a nurse and worked shifts, and even though my father had a day job, he started and finished early and I spent my early years being left with a babysitter – one that I was dropped off to before the sun rose every morning and picked up just before sunset. There were other children that my babysitter would look after, but I didn't have much in common with any of them and learnt to play games alone.

My parents were older than most of the other parents at school, and mine were the only ones that weren't Australian or white European. They were strict too. Overly strict and aside from already not fitting in, I had rules imposed on me that meant that I couldn't do even half the "normal" things that the other kids at school did, including being allowed to go on school camps... at least until I was halfway through high school.

I was taught, by example mostly, that a female had to do everything to maintain the household, but was not in charge of the finances or any big decisions. I was shown how she had a very specific role to play and that simply doing what you wanted to, was not an option. I was told to study hard, get a good job, find a husband and have a family. That was life. That's how it worked and any deviation from that plan would result in endless unhappiness.

So I studied hard, did as I was told, tried not to push any boundaries, but was still yelled at and blamed for things that I didn't do. I left home as soon as I could, found a job and started working. But that wasn't much better. I tried to be everything to everyone and it kept failing. I was never fulfilled in any job and tried many over the years. I received a lot of guidance in some and a lot of hard lessons in others.

I continued on the path that I was told to, even though I didn't like it. I got married, worked on my career some more (and finally started seeing some real results) and years later, had children. On the outside, it all looked perfect. Corporate career woman who frequently travelled, globally... married with children... always dressed in tailored suits and heels and never seen without her hair or make-up done... someone who looked like they had it all.

What a laughable illusion. If only everyone knew what happened behind closed doors, because somewhere along the way to this seemingly perfect life, over the years, little by little, I lost every bit of me by trying to exist and fit in.

Deep down, I was unhappy, unfulfilled, and in denial, because no matter what, I had my parents' voices in my head telling me that this was how it was and that you had to keep pushing through -no matter what- and most of all, to never give up on what you've built.

They were so wrong.

Part 3: Warning: System Malfunction

And then one day, it finally reached the point where it seemed like my body had given up on me and one of the biggest red flags in my relationship was thrown in my face.

I was at home with two of my young children and I had an anaphylactic reaction that resulted in my eyes puffing up to the point where I could barely see. I called my husband in a state of panic and he didn't seem bothered. He told me that it would be inconvenient for him to leave work to take me to the hospital.

As I was more worried about my children than myself, because I couldn't see enough to care for them and they were too little to do anything on their own, I didn't notice the red flag immediately. I also didn't realise that this was the start of an end.

Over the next few years, because of my health, I saw a number of specialists, the inside of the ER several times and took on endless advice that did more harm than good.

I suffered on a daily basis with weeping sores that were itchy, painful, and made me look like a disfigured monster. No doctor or specialist knew what was wrong and none of them could do or give me anything to make me better. In the end, it was my own elimination diet that uncovered a list of foods and ingredients that were making me sick, many of which weren't detected in my allergy tests.

So, I changed my entire diet and everything that came into contact with my skin. It was all surface level and it worked for a while. The rashes subsided and things went back to a type of normal. But the real cause went unnoticed: my own emotional unhappiness with major components of the life that I had created and was living, that had manifested itself into visible things that I could no longer ignore.

But because of what I was taught growing up, I kept fighting a losing battle and stayed in a relationship that I should have walked out on years prior. I missed several red flags that were actually flashing neon signs by then.

But my children noticed.

Whilst I was out shopping with them, two of my three children approached me and told me how they had written a list of traits that they wanted in a father. Amused, I entertained their idea by reading the list that they had brought with them, thinking that I'd talk to my husband later about how he could do some of what they'd written. The children told me that it wasn't an exhaustive list but I noticed that it did have more than a hundred things on it.

And as I read through the list of traits, I slowly realised that their father had none of them. More importantly, the list contained things that every child should be receiving from their father. But mine weren't. There was no quick discussion with my husband that could fix this.

Isn't it strange how there are some things that you can't unsee once you've opened your eyes to it? That when the hidden is known, all the signs become glaringly obvious, making you wonder how you could have ever missed them before?

That was when I gave my marriage one last big try.

When it didn't work, I figured that it'd be better to rebuild elsewhere than to stay... if not for my sake, for theirs.

Part 4:

The Secret Chaotic Storm

Words cannot describe the inner turmoil that I had... the guilt and shame for letting things go unnoticed... for failing as a parent, as a mother... wondering if I could really just do this all on my own, with my children in tow, and rebuild everything again. I was questioning whether things were bad enough to take it to the authorities. Everything was questioned by this stage, because it was difficult to keep things grounded when angry words were being said to me as I tried to make sense of everything and take steps to walk away.

But things were really bad and the authorities needed to be involved and I'm glad that I spoke up.

Acknowledging that there was a massive problem was my first step - and a huge step. Seeking help and assistance was my second. But the steps that came after were harder, because they were long and drawn out, dragging over years.

Leaving any relationship is difficult. Leaving one that I had invested so many years of my life in was traumatic. Rebuilding not just my life, but the lives of my children, after everything that each of us had endured, was probably my biggest test. And other step forward was met with a roadblock or detour.

Rebuilding your life and the foundations of who you are, who you want to be and where you're going, hits crazy levels when you have children in the equation. The decisions, the choices, the expenses, the compromises, the changes... they are all so much more complex. You can't just choose to go without because it impacts them. You can't just change suburbs without thinking about their school and their friends. In reality, this wasn't just about physically rebuilding. This was about their emotional and mental healing just as much as it was about mine.

My thoughts at that time were this: over all those years, if I had the strength to endure everything that I go through, then I have the strength to keep moving forward and to make things better. Because this time, I wasn't going to let myself or my children down.

Part 5: From Permission To Realisation To Change

When I gave myself permission to heal, and more importantly: permission to forgive myself for what had happened, knowing that I did the best thing I could have at the time, and that no amount of replaying any of the past events would change anything... that's when my ah-ha moments came rushing in, thick and fast.

That's when I realised that the things I experienced, as terrible as they were, were invaluable. I had gained perspectives and insights that couldn't be taught or learnt in textbooks. I had accumulated knowledge that only those who have gone through it themselves would know and understand. I also had unique ways of looking at those circumstances and seeing ways out that others didn't.

That's when I realised that I could teach this to others.

I know that there needs to be darkness before you can appreciate the light, and that everyone has lessons to learn in this lifetime, but no-one should have to stumble, fall and struggle through what I experienced on their own. No-one should ever feel completely isolated, exposed and raw, without someone being there to understand and help. I know that I wasn't the first to go through what I did, and I definitely won't be the last, but I can be the person that makes the difference to the next group of men and women who come up against even a fraction of the same issues and challenges that I did.

And so my focus became clear: Wellbeing Life Coaching.

Part 6: The Universe Has My Back

There's something magical about putting a request out to the universe, and then finding the exact thing (or person) that you asked for. That's how I found my first tribe of people who understood me and helped me get things off the ground, which included my first coach who believed in my abilities and didn't think I was off with the fairies. With them, I grew and evolved further. I reshaped various facets of myself and started sharing the knowledge with my clients. It was then that I really started to feel comfortable, and when things in my life started to really flow.

Doing what I'm passionate about and creating real change in the lives of others is uplifting, empowering and fulfilling. It flows effortlessly and makes my "work" feel more like fun rather than a chore. Every day feels authentic and unrestricted.

I spend my days working on various parts of my business including my time with clients, but because I enjoy it so much, my days really do fly by. My children benefit from me feeling and being happy and fulfilled. I have the time and patience to play with them and enjoy their company. We have time as a family to do things together every day, even if it's just talking, sharing bad jokes, playing a board game, or watching a movie. And I have time for me. I'm balanced now and it shows.

Roadblocks and detours show you that there are other ways of getting to where you want to go. They don't necessarily mean that you need to just stop or go back the way you came. Slowing down is not delaying – it's showing care in what you're doing and giving you time to do things thoroughly. Your life works on your timetable and whether you feel it or not, you are the one driving it.

Part 7: Happily Ever After

I can't tell you exactly how this story ends because it hasn't ended and I don't think it ever will: not even after I leave this lifetime. My story will go on living, breathing and evolving for years to come because I've started something big. I've started to make all the changes that I wanted to when I was a little girl, dreaming of how my life would be.

Admittedly, with all the nay-sayers, I never thought I'd get to where I am today and I certainly didn't anticipate half the journey that I went on, but...

I couldn't be where I am without it. I couldn't have the knowledge and first-hand experience without it. I wouldn't be able to teach my content to others without it. And I wouldn't be able to really understand the depths and the complications without it.

Everything that I have experienced has shown me my own strength, resilience, creativity and leadership. I've proved to myself how wonderful life can be if you just have faith in your own abilities, and it has trained me to lead others, in whatever setting or group size.

Where do I see myself tomorrow? I see myself travelling between shores and calling many places home, so I can reach, teach and help thousands in person. I see my children growing up and leading much easier lives because I've set the solid positive foundations for them. I see them continuing my legacy in their way.

And most importantly, I see you reading more about me and interacting with me in some way, whether that be in coaching sessions, an online course, a large speaking event, or through another book.

In the future, I see everything that I have created thus far flourishing further, blossoming brighter and penetrating past even the darkest corners of this world... making such a profoundly positive impact that it can't be ignored or silenced... just like I originally intended.

Part 8: The Lessons Condensed

My biggest lesson was to be yourself. Always. However, that may look. Don't worry about what other people think or say, because you'll be judged no matter what you do or don't do. In the end, their opinions don't matter because it's you that you have to live with every day for the rest of your life. if you're okay with the person that looks back at you in the mirror, then that's all that matters. It's not your job to make other people like you. They form their own opinions based on their own thoughts, fears and insecurities. Don't let it stop you. Being different allows you the space and motivation to find more creative solutions and workarounds.

Don't compare yourself to others ever. Don't look at how long it's taken others to do something and compare it to yourself. You have no idea what else is going on in their lives. It'll be different to yours. Guaranteed! Everyone has different circumstances and you need to make the most of the ones in your own path.

Change what you don't like and don't be afraid to just take a step and try. You never know what you can accomplish until you do. Every misstep is a lesson to take on and an opportunity to try again. You are the only person who is really stopping you.

Have your boundaries and stand by them, because your standards tell others what you will and won't accept from them. Be proud of who you are, what you've done and what you will do. Give yourself more credit and embrace every part of who you are, because you wouldn't be where you are now, without every little piece.

There is nothing you cannot do; I know that you are amazing. You can have it all – you can have the balanced life you always wanted. If you're ready, take my hand and I'll show you how.

> *"You are the only person who is really stopping you"* – Ana Angelique

Authentically,

Ana

Rediscovering the girl in the Yellow Tutu

To my partner Sean for making me laugh even when I don't want to and for being there to remind me that life doesn't always have to be so serious.
And to my mum and dad – Joe and Julie, for always being there to listen no matter what the distance was.

"We are all connected by a simple wish, to be visible, to be heard, to know that we matter" – Vlada Mars

I am a 44 year old recovering people pleaser and perfectionist, conquering the world of becoming visible.

For a long time, I didn't feel I belonged anywhere. I was a wanderer, didn't have a 10 year career plan, wasn't married, didn't have kids, hadn't bought my first home and spent way too much money on shoes. Everyone was telling me how I need to get my life in order. Sadly, I believed their opinions were more important than my own and my perception of myself decline over the years.

My best friend died when she was 38 years old. Far too young, so many adventures still to come.

Although there was so much the hurt and sadness, that day became the pivotal moment I decided I wanted my life to be different. It was the day I decided started say 'yes' to me.

I'd had a niggling feeling to start my own coaching business for some time. I was coaching people informally and loved it. My whole energy lifted when I saw I was making a difference to people's lives. I also had plenty of excuses as to why I couldn't or shouldn't do it. I was in my comfort zone having been in the corporate world for 20 years. I was afraid of the unknown and what was possible.

So I started investing in myself and did the inner work to rediscover who I was and what really mattered to me in life. I engaged a coach to help me work through how I was feeling and shift my mindset and perception of myself. I took ownership of the decisions I made and stepped back into the drivers seat of my own life.

I used to feel judged, lonely and invisible and now I don't. Now I believe in my value, worth and what I offer to the world around me. My story is one of personal development, transformation and change. I believe everyone has the ability to take the steps to become visible in their own world and live a life they truly love.

Welcome to my story about how I rediscovered the girl in the yellow tutu...

I grew up with my older brother in Cairns, Far North Queensland (some of you may know it as the gateway to the Great Barrier Reef) to kind, hard-working, determined parents. My dad ran a small house-building business and was a successful sportsman. My mum did everything for us and was a self-taught sewer, bookkeeper, and anything else she set her mind to.

When I was three months old, life wasn't travelling super well as I had an extreme eczema outbreak. I lived off a soy milk diet which was when my weight challenge began.

As I grew older, I had a very normal childhood hanging out with my cousins and friends. Overall, I was a pretty relaxed and calm kid. I was active, but as I was often reminded, I was chubby. Family members would constantly tell me I had put on weight or make comments about the way I looked. I went on my first diet when I was about 10 years old. You name the diet, I have probably tried it...

My ultimate dream was to be a ballerina. Dancing was my passion and I was good at it. When I was seven, I wore a bright yellow tutu which made me feel happy and alive. Dancing allowed me to escape reality, be creative, have freedom, and feel extraordinary and graceful.

I always thought dance was my saviour. I felt confident and comfortable. I felt at home and safe. I was my own person when I was on a stage. It was my happy place.

One day something changed. My dancing instructor started telling me how overweight I was compared to what dancers should look like. Mothers of other dance students would snicker behind my back and I was soon being excluded from group dances because the costume I had to wear didn't suit my body type.

Because of this, I quit dancing.

I convinced myself that other people were right. I wasn't supposed to be a ballerina because I didn't look like one. I didn't fit the criteria because I wasn't skinny enough. Those stories turned into me feeling like I wasn't good enough. I believed I should be part of the backstage crew rather than dancing front and centre on the stage. I was embarrassed and felt immense shame about what I looked like. I never saw myself as a success. In fact, I saw myself as a failure. My self confidence and self-esteem was low.

So at the age of 15, I let go of my dream and got lost in life as I tried to fit in rather than embrace who I was. I did what I thought everyone else expected me to do. I finished school, went to university, got a good, stable job. I tried dating but was always told I wasn't "marriage" material because I was overweight.

By the time I was 35, I didn't have huge savings in the bank because I had an addictive behaviour to spend money rather than save it as I searched for things to buy that made me feel good. Hence why I have an extensive shoe collection.

I was single, didn't own a house or have kids. I moved around a lot searching for a place to fit in. I punished my body by living an unhealthy lifestyle, I was very overweight, and worked extremely hard to be a success in my job to the point I continuously burnt myself out but kept going because I was trying to please everyone, be the good girl and do what I thought was expected.

Underneath all of that, happiness and all the things I loved about life had disappeared.

My best friend died suddenly when we were 38 years old. It absolutely rocked my world. I was in shock. At her funeral and wake, we celebrated the fun times and memories. It was there I saw the ripple effect of the amazing legacy she had left behind. She did this simply by being herself and doing what she loved.

This is when the first penny dropped for me. I wanted life to be different. I wanted to create my own legacy.

It was still some time before I really started taking action because I was scared of what life could look like.

The year I turned 40, I felt fat, awkward, self-conscious and judged by everyone especially myself. I didn't feel like I fitted in this world. I felt alone and lonely. I felt unloved and not worthy. I was unhappy, embarrassed and felt like I had let my own family down as I had failed them.

I criticised myself more than anyone else could. I had lost my confidence and questioned everything I did. I worried immensely and my anxiety levels skyrocketed.

All I wanted was for people to like me. I was frightened of upsetting, hurting and disagreeing with people. When I thought I had done something wrong, it would cause turmoil inside of me for days – sometimes even weeks and months. So I thought it was easier to sit in the background and hope I got through events unscathed. I tried to hide. I didn't want to stand out.

What had happened to me???

I had gone from this confident seven year old girl who loved dancing to the beat of her own drum in her yellow tutu to a scared 40 year old who felt trapped in life because she thought everyone hated her and she had nothing going for her. The seven year old girl was a stranger to 40 year old me.

This was when the second penny dropped and when I started taking action to transform my life. I recognised that I couldn't change the choices I had made, but I did have control over what choices I could make into the future. Instead of hiding from the world, I set out to find the girl in the yellow tutu so she would no longer be a stranger.

Over the last five years, I have invested in an immense amount of time, effort and money to find my path in life and I don't regret any decision I have made.

I guess some may say, when I turned 40, I had a mid-life crisis. I would rather call it my mid-life comeback!

My journey comprises of self-development, self-awareness, self-reflection and being curious. I learnt to recognise how many brave things I have already achieved in my life.

- At 15, I left an environment where I was being bullied for how I looked even though it meant giving up something I loved.
- I left home when I was 17 years old to go to university in a town 2000km away from my family.
- I moved cities four times by myself and rebuilt my life, career and friendship circles and networks.
- I put myself forward for promotions and new jobs as opportunities arose.
- I went on holidays, ate in restaurants and watched movies on my own.
- I tried online dating and met a dependable, trustworthy and kind man who I have now been with for 10 years.

- I have travelled the world, explored new places and met incredible people.
- I am a successful leader who has run numerous multi-million dollar teams.
- I took four months off work to care for my elderly parents, create new memories and reconnect given we had lived in different cities for 20 years.
- I resigned from a 20 year corporate career

I never saw myself as being brave until I took the time to reflect on what I have achieved. It's only been since I started to share my story that others have commented on how brave I am as for them, some of the things I have done are super scary.

Imposter syndrome, feelings of not being good enough, the fear of failure, the fear of success and becoming comfortable with being seen and heard were all hurdles I had to jump over and continue to jump over. The work doesn't stop once you have had your first or second breakthrough. I choose to invest in myself everyday to make sure I am continuing to strive for my goals and not allowing my inner critic to get the better of me.

The key lessons that have made my comeback successful are:
- Letting go of old stories that were not true or taking me in a direction based on fear and scarcity.
- Practicing self-compassion by forgiving others and most of all, forgiving myself.
- Recognising and being grateful for who I am and what I bring to the world rather than trying to fit in.
- Articulating what is important to me, what my non-negotiables are and what my personal values are.
- Letting go of the need to people-please and make everything perfect.
- Acknowledging the good moments in life rather than focussing on things that aren't going so well.

- Asking for help to stay on track.
- Remembering it takes time, effort and money to invest in yourself – nothing happens in five minutes, nor is it delivered to you on a silver platter.

As a result of all of this, I found the clarity, confidence, happiness and peace to live my best life on my terms. Best of all, I found the seven year old girl in the yellow tutu. She was always there. She was just hiding backstage.

My vision and mission is simple – to empower others to embrace their unique self and become visible by taking action, stop hiding in the shadows and start living their best life.

In 2021, I founded my own coaching business helping individuals, leaders, and teams discover how they can be seen, heard and valued in their world.

Outwardly, you may appear successful yet inwardly, your self-belief and worth may have disappeared and you feel invisible, not heard and not valued. You might be on the treadmill heading towards burnout, overwhelm and loneliness.

These are the people I want to work with. These are the people I want to help so they can shift onto the path of freedom, happiness, and peace.

Transformation takes commitment. Whether you are a leader of teams, a business owner, a corporate professional, a person trying to get back into the workforce, or a person wanting to redesign what your future life looks like, it's not too late to say 'yes' to your dreams.

There is no one-size-fits-all. Everyone's journey is different. This is why I am passionate about and love coaching people. Once you start to see, hear and believe in yourself, you will wonder why you waited so long to start.

Reflecting on my comeback journey, my top three light bulb moments to inspire others to become visible are:

1. Find your voice from within and believe in yourself

We are all amazing individuals. We all have something to contribute to the world. Some of us don't know what that is. Others feel like they know what they want to say but they either don't feel heard, or they don't know how to express it. This is scary to admit and it's easier to deflect and blame others. If we dig deep, do the work, and find our voice, we can clearly articulate what we can offer the world and what we want from the world. We rediscover what is important and valuable to us. We rediscover who we are. The process is messy, uncomfortable, and overwhelming but it is one of the most rewarding things you can do. If you aren't sure where to start, engage a coach or mentor to guide you through the journey.

2. Speak from the heart, share your experience and be part of the conversation

When I found my voice and started sharing my perspectives and experiences aka my personal and professional life journey, I received messages from people, some who I knew and others I didn't, telling me that my messages resonated, and it felt like I was writing about them. I spoke from the heart and people wanted to know how they could do what I did. Knowing that your voice and messages can create conversations of inspiration and hope for others. Try starting a conversation with someone about something you are passionate about and by sharing your story, you too can create a ripple effect of change.

3 Connect and learn

A major part of becoming visible is connecting with and learning from others. Connect with people in your community, join a mentoring group, listen to podcasts, read books, reach out to someone who inspires you and ask to have a chat with them. Being around like-minded people who have been on the journey you are on will inspire and push you to be better - they will encourage you to take the next scary step. They will be your champion, confidant, and cheerleader. They will challenge you to think bigger and differently. You want different perspectives and people in your corner. At the same time, there are going to be others who you will let go of, and that is okay. It's all part of the process.

"Be yourself. Everyone else is already taken"
                                        Oscar Wilde

With much gratitude

Kylie xx

Lisa Ohtaras

Energy Healer, Soul Healer, Intuitive Spiritual Coach, Spiritual Educator, Reiki Master, Seichim Master, Medium, Channel & Soulful Forgiveness Workshop Facilitator, Australia.

The Spiritual Journey and Evolution of the Soul

To all the Ascended Masters, The Divine, and My Higher Self, I am eternally grateful for your teachings, guidance, unconditional love, support, my spiritual gifts & the work I conduct. Thank you!

Thank you to all my family, friends, soul sisters, soul brothers, and clients who have assisted me on my spiritual journey to date and continue to assist me. You all know who you are! I am very grateful!

And thank you dear dad for sharing your knowledge relating to the significance of forgiveness. I love you. Rest in Peace.

"We are more than our name, personality, and physical body"
Lisa Ohtaras

I was born in Australia to Italian immigrant parents and grew up in Southern Sydney in New South Wales, Australia.

As early as five years of age, I dreamed of being a nurse helping people who were sick. Both my parents made it crystal clear they were not in favour of me pursuing nursing as my career. However, I followed my dream and studied and trained to become a registered nurse. As time progressed both my parents saw and understood the blessing relating to me being a healer at the core of my being.

Working as a Registered Nurse for over twenty years provided me with a helpful foundation and the people skills for the future work I would conduct as an Energy Healer, Soul Healer, Mentor, Coach, Educator and more.

My life script and Sacred Contract were meticulously constructed by my Soul prior to my birth.

I married the man I fell deeply in love with, and we had two beautiful children, our son and our daughter. Our marriage had its highs and lows. Our family unit shared many magnificent times and not so happy ones.

I appeared to have it all, yet my physical body failed me...

Although I appeared to have it all in the physical world; an amazing supportive family, the beautiful dream home, working in the career of my choice - halfway into my marriage, my health became seriously compromised.

My **SOUL** created multiple health challenges at one time.
I called my naturopath to go and see her for help, but she was away on holidays. So, I contacted another highly recommended naturopath whom I'd never met before, who sensed my fear and despair and booked my appointment to see her immediately.

Following her assessment, I was informed I had the warning signs of Multiple Sclerosis (M.S.) which is an autoimmune disease. M.S. was then incurable and to this day remains incurable by traditional medicine.

The naturopath gave me a protocol to follow which included plenty of rest, minimal work, vitamin supplements and herbal teas. I scheduled another appointment to see her one month later.

Following the instructions were easy for me as I was determined to become well again, restore my good health, and resume normal life. I rested during that month more than I had rested in many previous years.

When I returned for my second visit, I was devastated to hear that my condition had become worse even though I had strictly adhered to the naturopath's instructions

The pain, numbness, alternating with pins and needles in my arms and hands, feet and limbs had all become exacerbated and were more troublesome. And so were the many other symptoms such as night sweats, insomnia, chronic fatigue and visual challenges. Never did I imagine that day would be so significant and of great importance for my future.

Growth, inner work is the prelude to the light at the end of the dark tunnel...

It was on that same day, following so much crying that there were no more tears left inside my being, that I made the conscious connection with my Spirituality and connected with the Angelic realm.

The Angelic beings of light informed me my health was seriously compromised. I was guided not to take medicines. Instead, I was to do Spiritual growth to heal my body.

The Angelic beings of illuminated light guided my growth and what I should do. Many years of holding onto imploding negative emotions when I was unhappy, had contributed to the health challenges I was experiencing.

Following their guidance and diligently committing to doing the inner work, I noted a distinct observation. There was a profound change in my mindset. My thought processes became more positive while I was doing the work and after the completion of the work.

Whilst I was taking the supplements from the naturopath, my mindset had not changed whatsoever. The energy of a serious illness will not transform with the same thoughts that created the energy and illness. That is why there was no improvement in my symptoms or illness.

In fact, my symptoms had worsened which I had explained to me by my Soul, was purposely created by my Soul to instigate my conscious connection with my Spirituality. My Soul succeeded with their master plan strategy to awaken me.

My spiritual awakening and path to living consciously...

I learned during my spiritual awakening that I was more than my name, my personality and my physical temple which houses my Soul. I learnt that inner work is required by everybody. Our Soul wants inner work to be done and there are so many reasons why, some of which I'll explain.

The Soul is seeking expansion of consciousness, to heal past lives (many millions of people on planet Earth have had multiple lifetimes), for the person to connect with their inner self, to learn to harness the energy from within, learn who they really are, make the connection with their inner selves and access universal wisdom from within.

Additionally, we are meant to connect with our spiritual gifts and abilities and use those abilities to make a positive difference wherever possible, and to discover our Soul Purpose also known as the Sacred Contract and fulfil that purpose.

My learnings were life-changing to say the least. I attended and engaged in many courses which collectively helped me to heal from within.

I learnt the importance and power of forgiveness of other people and of myself, it was a significant part of my healing journey. **Major forgiveness work helped heal my body which was out of balance and out of alignment.**

Following my late father's transition, he reiterated what I already knew relating to the power of forgiveness. **Letting go of emotions and forgiveness of other people and oneself is a major component of healing from within.**

During this lifetime every person will at some point experience a personal Spiritual awakening. We may not initially recognize what the Soul is doing, as was the case for me.

The person's Soul will then create another situation to instigate the awakening to transpire. The cycle continues for the duration as required by the Soul, until the person awakens. Life lessons become more complicated, health challenges and illnesses are amplified in severity, repeating patterns become more intensified, relationship problems can become quite troublesome and financial challenges can become more exacerbated.

Other situations are also created by the Soul to awaken the individual. Awakenings created by the Soul will manifest in different forms. One may experience for example an illness, an accident, a major trauma, a near death experience during a hospital admission or during a surgical procedure, the loss of a loved one just to name a few, or a person may organically awaken to the truth within them, resulting from the right circumstances and conditions being in alignment.

How I healed from within...

I restored my good health and wellbeing through daily meditation, personal and spiritual growth, letting go and major forgiveness and self-forgiveness. It took me two years without the use of any medication whatsoever to heal. My Soul was rejoicing whenever I did inner work. Determination to have well-being reigned in me.

The Soul is recreating their energy and past timelines through a person's Spirit (the physical entity part of the person), which allows us to feel the energy and have the experiences. Why? So, the person can feel it to heal it.

Metaphysical knowledge fascinated me; I acquired an insatiable appetite to learn more.

Following my inner healing when my health had been restored, I connected with the Spirit world, helping Spirits who were not at peace. Through my mediumship I wrote transcripts for their loved ones and conveyed messages of closure to help people.

During this period of growth my husband and I grew apart. After thirty years of marriage, we separated and subsequently divorced. Following inner work and spiritual growth, we both have an amicable relationship.

My nursing career continued for a few more years following my inner healing journey, during which I also worked with the Spirit world. Then I decided to explore Energetic Healing further. I studied the Diploma of Energetic Healing at college and loved every module and lesson.

The end of my much-loved nursing career to a more rewarding and fulfilling career...

During my studies at college, I was Divinely guided to cease my two-decade long nursing career and commence living and working my Soul Purpose, my Sacred Contract.

I was reluctant to leave nursing because I loved the career. Helping people is my passion, making a positive difference to people's lives is what drives me.

The Divine reassured me I would love the next phase of my life and they were one hundred percent correct. I love fulfilling my Sacred Contract.

I started my business Caring Energetic Healing almost two decades ago and I have had the privilege and wonderful opportunity to facilitate the transformation of energy at a Soul level for my clients. This sacred work is what I was born to do on planet Earth.

My work takes place in one-to-one sessions, group work and remote sessions anywhere in the world. When working with clients, I utilize 43 years of my experience combining my medical background, Energetic Healing studies and learnings from my own healing journey learnt directly from Ascended Masters, The Divine and my Higher Self. The work I conduct allows me to help people to ascend to the next levels of their evolution.

The results have been positively life changing for people's health, well-being, improved relationships with themselves and other people and much more. There have been so many incredible, amazing miracles.

The energetic healing work I conduct clears blocked energy and negative energies, including energy from past lives, ancestral influences, familial and ancestral karmic debt, core negative beliefs, limitations, fears, anxiety, poverty consciousness and more.

I conduct Soul healing, including Soul Retrievals, to transform energy at a Soul level and clear future negative timelines created by the Soul (energy which is not conducive to well-being and happiness).

My mentoring and coaching help to heal emotions and traumas at a Soul level.

Through my mediumship work I help to clarify a person's Life Purpose and Sacred Contract.

I am also a Soulful Forgiveness Facilitator, helping people to forgive themselves and others. To let go of emotions that no longer serve them at the point of creation where the energy originated. It is deeply transformative for betrayal issues, separation, divorce, love matters of the heart and any held resentments.

In addition to helping human beings to have inner peace through Soulful Forgiveness work, I have also assisted troubled spirits who have passed over, who were grief-stricken with negative emotions and unforgiveness issues.

When living in human form on planet Earth, the person was not ready to let go of issues and forgive people and themselves. Following the death of their physical human form, the spirits were guided to me via their living relatives, clients I work with, or people who know of me and the nature and quality of work I conduct.

Forgiveness and self-forgiveness are major components of healing a serious illness ...

Through my mediumship, this information was channeled through me to my mother and sister from my late father Michele, two days following his transition to the spirit world. He requested I share this story to assist people.

My late father passed over in 2007 following 26 months of having bowel and liver cancer. Initially Michele had surgery after being diagnosed with a mass in his abdominal area. Following the surgery, he was diagnosed with bowel cancer and liver cancer.

The professor of surgery informed Michele, in the presence of all four daughters, he would have six months maximum to live if he did not have further surgery to his liver. The choice was made exclusively and solely by my father, not to pursue further surgery or have chemotherapy for cancer.

Alternatively, Michele selected to have regular energetic healing and soul healing sessions conducted by me. He also had two naturopath visits for herbal remedies.

Together, my father and I did deep forgiveness work. He felt well, looked amazing, had high energy levels and had very minimal pain during the duration of his illness.

During the last few weeks of my father's life, he experienced pain. The major challenge which adversely affected my father was the food restrictions due to cancer. My father gave up the will to live, retracted the forgiveness he had done and stated, "I want to die."

Whilst my mother was having an energetic healing two days following my father's transition, he channeled through me to my mother and sister. My father was remorseful and angry.

He was remorseful about his past actions. Following my father's transition, the Divine informed him that, had he not retracted the forgiveness work he had done and remained in alignment with living, he would still be living with his family on Planet Earth and not in the spirit world.

Always remember the power of forgiveness.

My parting gift...

My spiritual journey has taught me beneficial wisdom I would like to share:

1. You are more than your name, personality, and nationality. You are the collective consciousness, the total of everything you have been throughout history. We are on Earth as physical beings to heal the Soul, expand the Soul's consciousness, discover, and fulfil your Soul's Purpose, and help the evolution of planet Earth.
2. The Soul is creating situations, circumstances, conditions, and events for us to learn, grow, heal from within, transform and evolve our Spirit and our Soul.
3. The agreement was made prior to birth, do the inner work, and heal from within. Let go of everything and every person you are not at peace with.
4. Everything which transpires in your life is done for you, not to you.
5. All challenges and unpleasant circumstances are growth opportunities.
6. Your Soul is recreating past energy and timelines to allow the person to have awareness. Feel it to heal it.
7. Your physical body is the barometer to your Soul.
8. If you are ill with a serious illness, the thoughts and emotions which created the illness, require change for positive transformation of energy. Inner work complemented with energy healing are highly beneficial for the positive transformation of energy.

9. Forgiveness of other people and acceptance and self-forgiveness are major components of transforming energy for a serious health condition and all other illnesses.

10. The SOUL-U-TIONS are within you. The Soul created the energy and will dissipate the energy when the inner work is carried out by the person.

"There is a spiritual SOUL-U-TION to every challenge and problem." - Lisa Ohtaras

Infinite blessings,

Lisa Ohtaras

Aspire to Inspire

"Within our dreams and aspirations, we find our opportunities"
Sugar Ray Leonard

Do you remember when you were a child, so many adults would ask you the same question? "What are you going to be when you grow up?" WOW!

How did you know the answer? You were only a child, and may not have even started school. I know when I was little, I really didn't have any idea, yet I mostly answered, "A Teacher." Why? Because I knew what a teacher was, and what they did. They taught you things, lots of things: like reading, writing and arithmetic. The other idea I had, I wanted to write a book. I didn't know at the time about fiction and non-fiction, and genres, or who my audience would be. But it was my dream.

I grew up in rural/remote Queensland. At that time, most women didn't work if they had children. My mum was different. She went back to work not long after I started school, as my parents had bought into a dry-cleaning business. Just mum and dad to do all the work. Even after they sold the business, Mum stayed on as an employee. When we moved to the city, she obtained work in clerical administration, and continued for over 20 years.

Until we moved to the city, I thought women could work in the bank, in retail, in an office, be a nurse or be a teacher. There were not a lot of opportunities in small country towns. But in the city, there were so many more. And women could go to university, some even got trades training and some stayed in the more traditional 'female' roles.

When I had completed my senior schooling, I had a number of opportunities for employment. I had been working in a film laboratory and was offered a permanent role. I had passed the bank and public service exams, and I had achieved a Tertiary Entrance Score providing an opportunity to go into Special Education. I'd always said I wanted to be a teacher, remember. There was another opportunity I had, to enlist in the Women's Royal Australian Air Force (WRAAF). I had options.

I chose to join the WRAAF and signed my life to Queen and Country for a period of three years. This meant I had to leave home, my family and the state I had been born and bred in. My life was uplifted and transported interstate.

This was the start of my career, or rather, employment journey as an adult. I had held many positions prior to leaving school which included tea and tidy in a hairdressing salon; a clipper in a hat factory, sheet factory and men's clothing factory; check-out chick at Coles Supermarket and an office assistant where my mum worked.

I stayed in the Air Force for three years and seven months. During that time, I had resided at Tottenham (Melbourne), Wagga Wagga (NSW), Point Cook (Melbourne) and Werribee (Melbourne). I had met and married my husband, who was also in the Air Force. When I discharged from defence, I worked in retail, again at Coles Supermarket.

We moved to Ipswich, and I worked in Truck and Tractor Spares and hardware retail. We had two sons, and then moved to Darwin, where I began working for Westpac. I continued working for them for almost fourteen years, and was able to transfer when we moved to Wagga Wagga, Newcastle and Brisbane. At each branch I worked in, I was called upon to train new staff, and train existing staff when new procedures were introduced. I had never had any formal training in the area, yet I was able to conduct training sessions and achieve the required outcomes. There's that teacher my younger self had aspired to.

When I eventually departed from the bank, I moved into Youth Work where I was working with young people transitioning from formal schooling into further education, training or employment. This was one of the most satisfying positions I held.
In my role as a transition officer, I became a teacher, a mentor, a role model, and a confidante. I am so grateful to, and for, all the young people I met and worked with over a period of five years. They taught me so much, and I hope and trust I had a positive influence on their lives. I know I did for many, as they were not shy in telling me.

I worked with one young man who wanted to be an electrician. When apprenticeships were being advertised, I contacted him to let him know I had information he needed to come and get. He took it home and read it, and came back to me a few days later to tell me he couldn't apply. He felt he did not meet the criteria, as Maths B was a desirable element. When we discussed it, he met all the other criteria, and he had achieved Very High gradings in all his subjects. He submitted an application, phoned me when he got a call to attend a group interview and we made time to discuss the process. He was successful in that, got a call back for an individual interview, and we developed a strategy for that. He was successful, and got a call back to attend a medical. We were both feeling fairly confident at this stage.

I received a call from him late one afternoon, just prior to him finishing school. He was so excited; he couldn't wait to tell me his news. He had been offered an apprenticeship with the state government, in the electrical field of work, and would commence early in January. His mother later told me she found out he was successful when he phoned me. I was so grateful for that young man for trusting in me, to guide his potential future. Almost 20 years later, he is still employed in the field of work he was focused on when still at school.

I had a parent contact me some years after their son had left school, to thank me. Her son had failed year 9 and year 10, and was back at school to do year 11. School was not the place for him.

I spoke with this young man, the school and his parents. The only thing this boy would achieve by staying at school, was a piece of paper to say he attended. With the cooperation of the school and his parents, I was able to arrange some work experience and a modified school timetable. The employer saw his potential and offered him some part-time paid work, which developed into a traineeship and then an apprenticeship. He became a qualified fitter and welder, and eventually landed a position in Western Australia with a national company building boats. Hence, his mother's call to say thank you.

There were many stories like these, as young people learn differently and need different support and encouragement along the way. Sometimes school is not their best option. They need guidance, support, and mentoring.

> *"The greatest inspiration you can ever get is to know that you are an inspiration to others. Wake up and start living an inspirational life today"* - Unknown

I transitioned from youth work into the public service, where I was then overseeing organisations working in the youth transitions space. That too, was rewarding, as I had worked at the coal face and understood the challenges organisations faced when dealing with young people and the obstacles some had to overcome.

My supervisor would often ask how my organisations continually met their targets and the outcomes for young people. It was because I worked with them, to ensure their data was captured correctly, the methods they were using were appropriate, and the recording of outcomes met the criteria of the program. Guidance, support and mentoring.

I applied for and accepted a redundancy package as the youth programs were decommissioned. I was expected to work in an area I was totally unfamiliar with, and the support for my transition was not provided. The environment became toxic, for a number of reasons, and I decided I could no longer work under those circumstances.

I took time for me. For almost twelve months, I didn't want to face people at all. My self-esteem and self-worth had taken a hit. I needed to get better and heal my soul, my mind and my body.

I started volunteering and giving back to my community. I took on a position as a reading assistant at my grandson's school, to help children increase their reading capability. My grandson had lived in our house from birth to 18 months, and each night I would read to him. He was a very capable reader and had good comprehension. Unfortunately, others in his class were unable to read basic three letter words. This broke my heart. What gave me joy was to see these children improve their reading throughout the year, and being capable of reading books at a higher standard than at the beginning of the year.

The local Neighbourhood Centre was seeking volunteers and I applied. I became a literacy tutor for a lady who could speak English and understand spoken English, yet could not read or write in English. She was able to identify individual letters when we started, and twelve months later she was recognising words, able to read and write sentences and with assistance, read a low-level book. It is so rewarding to see the difference encouragement and support can make to another's life.

When I was well enough to step back into living, I undertook and completed studies to become a Life Coach. And I loved it. I started my own business and connected with some wonderful people. I was able to share my learnings with others; plan, develop and facilitate workshops; and continue my own growth as a coach.

During my studies, I met many mentors. One, in particular, was an author who assisted others in writing their own books. We were chatting one day and I told her my childhood dream of becoming a writer. Isn't it interesting the paths our lives take us on?

I told her it was time. She asked me "Why now?"

The answer was easy. I had run out of excuses. I had the time, I was financially able to do so, I had support, I knew I could write (wasn't sure how well), and I wanted to leave a legacy for my children and grandchildren. I also wanted my mum to be able to read it, before her illness took her from us.

"My Time to Shine" was written whilst doing my mentor's 90-day training course. I started her course on 1 July, and published my book on 30 September. My actual writing days were actually less than 30, as I kept a writing journal to keep track of my progress. I had achieved my dream; I was a published author.

Twelve months later, I was invited to be a contributing author to a compilation book – "Business Warriors – Taking Care Of Working Women In The 21st Century", where my chapter was titled "Reality: Check", where I discussed how our perceptions affect our outlook and our outcomes.

I had started my own meet-up group, Women Embracing Business, where I facilitated a monthly group meeting with the intention of offering support, encouragement and collaboration to those who attended. I am very proud to say, I maintained the group for three years before passing the reins to another beautiful woman. Within the group, many new connections were made, friendships blossomed, new ventures were commenced and many successful collaborations emerged.

For something different, I completed speaker training where I was on stage for five minutes (three times during the training) in front of 30 people I didn't know. I decided to really put myself out there, and signed up for IGNITE Brisbane, where I presented to 80 people I didn't know. But oh, what a buzz!!!

Life has a way of telling you to slow down. An event may impact, your situation changes, you may suffer loss and grief. Let me tell you, when all of these happen in a short space of time, you finally get the message.

My mum had been unwell and struggling with dementia for some years. Sadly, two years ago, she passed away. A few months later, my husband was made redundant from his job of seven years. We looked upon this as an opportunity to take some travel time. We booked a number of holidays, thinking we were finally going to live the retiree lifestyle. Oh no, the universe had something else in store, not only for us, but the whole world. Yep, you guessed it. A month after we had booked our travel, a world pandemic hit. All of our travel was cancelled.

What to do now? I had stepped back from my business when mum passed, and was only just starting to find my feet, by completing some short courses and getting my head back in the game. How many blows do you take before you take notice? Okay universe, I'm getting the message, loud and clear. Time to step back, reassess and reset.

Two writing opportunities presented themselves to be a contributing author to a compilation book. "Change Makers" provided an opportunity to tell my story of how I had had an impact on or influenced others. I was able to share my experiences of how my meetup group began, how it developed through time and the wonderful outcomes achieved. I had never had my own business previously, so I was learning along and through the journey. The group shared many wonderful moments.

The other opportunity was "I Did It", sharing another story around mindset. My contribution was "I Can Run." I shared how I had gone from being someone who didn't run, unless it was to save myself, to running half marathons in my mid-fifties. I had to change my mindset to achieve my outcome. It was not only my body that had to do the work, it was predominantly my mind. I had to look at and change my beliefs about my abilities and capabilities, my nutrition and hydration, the shoes and the clothes I wore, my training schedules and importantly, who I needed to support me. My journey inspired some of my friends who supported me whilst running as they too took up the challenge and went on to compete in future events.

Then along came more writing opportunities.

I wrote a case study for "Co-Create Your Dreams", due to be published early next year.

I write a bi-monthly article for an online magazine, "The Disruptive Publisher", on Happiness.

Two more compilation books presented themselves, "Mothers Making a Difference" and "Forever Changed by Suicide". In Mothers, I talk about "Who Am I?" as many women label themselves and is how they identify. My contribution discusses how we play many roles and take on many responsibilities throughout our life, and those roles have made us who we are, yet they do not define us. We are all so, so much more than a label and we need to be proud of who we are and what we have achieved. Empowering women to own their potential, and make a difference in the lives of others.

In the other book, it is a very personal story. I lost my brother to suicide almost 30 years ago, and I still grieve my loss today. My story shares how his passing impacted me. I cannot tell his story; I can only share mine. We need to be able to talk about this subject without shame, blame or guilt. If my story can ease the pain of others, my job is done.

I decided I wanted to do more with my writing and for some time, I have been interested in ghostwriting. I found a group to follow, then joined. The principal of the group was going to run a live training on Facebook. He is based in America, I had to work out the time differences, and I was able to attend. By the end of the training, I was hooked and enrolled in his course.

I put it out to the universe and within a week, I had a few enquiries, generally finding out what it meant and how it would work. And then, I was contacted by a potential client to write her story as a non-fiction memoir. We met, and are now working together to get her story told. Another contact has enlisted my services to write her story.

Through my writing adventures, I have worked with a number of editors and publishers. One publisher requested we catch up, to determine if there was a potential for collaboration. For now, I am writing manuscripts, and then I will refer my clients to editors and publishers. In the future, collaborations with editors and publishers will be another opportunity for me to grow. In the meantime, I am happy to take referrals from colleagues, publishers, editors and friends.

So much for my childhood dream of wanting to write a book. I have my own book, six compilations and two ghostwriting clients. Luckily, fortunately, gratefully, I thoroughly enjoy writing. It hasn't stopped there. I now have three other compilation books on the go, where I am writing a chapter on gratitude, a mother's journey and this chapter on inspiration.

I have constantly been learning throughout my life. As a young girl, I was an avid reader, and I still am today. I usually have two books on the go at the same time. Each morning, I read a personal/professional development style book, and of an evening, I will read a fiction novel. I have been a beta reader for other authors, and this too, helps me become a better writer.

Through my reading, training, self-development, and my learnings, I hope and trust I have inspired, and still can, inspire others to have faith in themselves to live their life on purpose, and enjoy each and every moment.

"My mission in life is not merely to survive, but thrive"
Maya Angelou

Broken to be Brilliant

The Potter and his blue bowl

The potter gazed lovingly at their finished work of art. The blue bowl was perfect in every sense of the word, perfectly crafted from premium clay, the potter had taken the time to make sure every aspect of their creation was perfect, from the smooth flat bottom to the delicate curves of the sides as they rose in splendour. A delicate blue glaze had turned this bowl from the ordinary to the extraordinary where it now sat being admired by its creator. Very delicately the potter lifted the bowl from the glazing plate and gave it pride of place in the shop window, front and centre where it could be admired day in and day out by customers as they browsed through the potters' wares looking for the perfect piece.

It wasn't too long after this that a young Mum and her son came in the shop in a flurry. All day the young Mum had been running late, from the moment her feet hit the floor it felt as though one thing after ran together to put her perfectly planned day out of sync so by the time she entered the shop her patience, already thin, had been stretched bare. Without thinking she let go of her young son's hand just long enough to adjust her shopping bags and it was in that instance that the young boy who had only just found the joy of walking on two legs took off across the shop. It was almost as though time slowed down. Mum dropped her bags and took off after him, the potter seeing what was happening also made a beeline for the young boy.

As though spurred on by the chase the boy ran faster and faster until he couldn't, and it was at that exact moment that he stopped having run headfirst into the display holding the potters prized blue bowl.

With bated breath, it felt like the entire shop stopped to watch as the bowl teetered precariously tipping back and forth before finally crashing to the floor shattering in pieces around the young boys' feet. In an instant the young Mum scooped the boy up and uttered a few words of reprimand before turning the potter to apologise. He was already on the floor carefully picking up the pieces of the broken blue bowl, he glanced up and her and smiled and in his gentle way assured her that all was ok, that this could be rectified. Seeing all the broken pieces in the potters hands the young Mum thanked him for his generosity in spirit and placating words for what she was sure was a lost cause and hurried out the door, now even more behind than when she had come in.

That night late, after the store had closed for the day and the frantic pace of retail life had ceased the potter sat down in his workshop and opened the cloth holding the pieces of his prized blue bowl. Carefully sorting them out as though they were an intricate puzzle, he laid them in order across his desk. All night he worked buzzing back and forth from his locked office to the furnace and back to his workshop until finally as the sun came up, he was finished.

Not long after, the young Mum having taken a moment while her son was sleeping, sat down with the newspaper. She flipped casually through the news before an article in the arts and entertainment section caught her eye. There was a half-page photo of the potter, the same kind elderly gentleman who had shown her so much grace, smiling proudly as he held in his hands an award for the highest honour a potter can receive. Beside him, the award-winning piece, a delicate blue glazed bowl pieced together with shards of gold now running through it where the cracks from the fall had once been. A bowl that had been destined for the scrap heap now taking out the highest accolades. For the potter instead of putting it out on the scrap heap had lovingly pieced together all the broken pieces and glued them together with gold he had smelted in his furnace. Turning his prized blue bowl into a priceless work of art.

Why being broken isn't the end

What is being broken? For some of us it may be the crashing of dreams in pieces at our feet, for others it may be losing our health or relationships we held dear. For others it may be being stripped bare of everything that made us who we are, our job, our home, our family. Whatever it is, being broken sucks. It hurts, it can be painful, embarrassing, filled with shame, self-doubt, fear, anger and loneliness. Being broken feels like the end of the world, the full stop after a particularly bad sentence. The end.

From a young age being broken was all I knew. Countless hours were spent curled up in emotional agony behind my bedroom door as life raged ranged around me. Leaving home at 17 I moved from one crisis to the next as I embraced my broken identity. What I didn't realise was that each event rather than tearing me apart was actually preparing me for something better, something bigger, something I could never see coming.

I watched out window as the tow truck reversed up our driveway, tucked away behind the curtain I hid my face in the soft lace material and watched the weathered face of the tow truck driver as he hitched my car to the tray and started the winching process. This was it; this was my rock bottom. I had worked so hard to put a roof over my family's head, food on the table and petrol in that car and yet despite my striving it wasn't enough. After falling behind on our payments, the car was finally being repossessed. That was it, this was the end. No car meant no transport which meant no job. Of course, no job meant no money which would make paying rent and keeping a roof over my family's head even harder. I was tired and worn out. As primary carer for my husband who had a disability and my wheelchair bound mother-in-law who battled an ongoing drug addiction, I was done. Mentally, physically, and emotionally. I was ready for the scrap pile; I was checking out.

I had spent the night before up at the hospital as my mother-in-law in a drug stupor, had fallen face first out of her wheelchair and had broken her nose.

Resisting the ambulance and police who arrived, I had to get her up off the floor and up to emergency and having a car was vital to making sure she could access the medical support she needed.

I watched as the tow truck left and sat sobbing in the lounge, feeling like I was 10 all over again, nothing had changed. Different crisis but same broken pieces falling across the floor of my heart.

It took a while, but that moment was a turning point for my life. Bit by bit I picked those broken pieces up and carried them around with me, starting what I know now to be my healing process. I thought at the time that being broken was the end. I couldn't see any way out. What point was there to continue when broken was all I was.

What I know now is that being broken isn't the end. In fact, being broken can quite often be the starting point for something new, something even greater to blossom. That it is from the place of brokenness that hope arises.

Once I had decided that my broken pieces needed to be put back together, there was an element of trust that needed to follow. I needed to trust that my ashes could be replaced with beauty, that healing was possible, and that change was real.

Ironically enough, being broken can bring hope, after all once we hit rock bottom, the only way is up, right? I'm not sure if it was emotional overwhelm or just plain exhaustion but as I sat in the lounge after the car had been taken, I remember laughing hysterically as I thought to myself, 'well Carolyn at least you can get that SUV you always wanted!'. What I didn't realise at the time was that thought that crazy hysterical thought was actually a seed, a small seed, of hope. Hope that things can and will get better. Hope that there is a future and a way forward. Today as I jump into my car which I paid outright for in cash and enjoy all its bells and whistles I think back to that day and smile.

What I was learning was that through being broken I was learning to firstly trust that something better could and would happen, I then started to have hope that things would start change and finally I developed resourcefulness to give my trust and hope legs and to put the healing process into action.

Being broken creates resourcefulness

One of my favourite TV shows growing up was MacGyver. Now I may be showing my age a little here, but boy did I love nothing more than behind glued to the TV watching as he figured his was out of yet another sticky situation with nothing more than a paperclip and a ball of string. If there was one word to describe MacGyver it would be resourceful. He knew how to use what he had on hand to shape his future and to give him a way forward... quite often through an open window at the bad guy's expense!

It's this same resourcefulness that being broken develops in us. Finding ways to work with what we have on hand to help create a better future only happens when being resourceful is all we have.

Once I knew that I was no longer content to continue to live broken, that I trusted that things could change and started hoping, I now needed to find way to make this happen. I scoured the internet for resources on healing, I spent time with people who had the maturity to speak into my life, I took time to work on my spiritual and emotional growth and started the forgiveness process. I looked for any opportunity to heal. Most mornings I was up before the sun walking through the streets with my earphones in. I listened to everything from the Bible (which was a must) through to Napoleon Hill, Marcus Aurelias, and the works of the Stoics. I was like a sponge. I listened and I learned. I used what resources I had available; which at that point was two legs, a phone, and data to start my healing process and to begin the move from brokenness to healing.

To this day I'll still go back and listen to those books refreshing my mind and my spirit and remind myself just how being broken ended up saving my life.

Being broken shapes and moulds our character

One thing that no one ever talks about when discussing brokenness is how lonely it actually is. I remember vividly sitting in the lounge of a friend's house having coffee listing to the conversation around me. Topics jumped from the boys fishing trip to the new mops the girls were trying out on their tiled floors. I painted on a smile, you know the one where you look interested, a little amused but not too committed that they would actually ask for your feedback! If only they knew! There was no way my husband would be able to make it out on a fishing trip and I was still reusing the same black and gold mop I bought when I was married as paying the bills was my first priority! I remember feeling in that moment an overwhelming sense of loneliness and isolation.

That experience stuck with me and even to this day I look for ways to engage with people on a deep and meaningful level, to make sure that my conversation and my words are thoughtful and seasoned with grace, that I am aware that not everyone I meet is in the same place as me. If I hadn't had been through the breaking process myself, I wouldn't have the same insight that I have today to be mindful of each person that I meet.

Quite often it is the people who have been broken that bring to the table the grace, wisdom and understanding that hurting people need. They bring that because they know what it's like to be broken and through that process it has shaped their character to be more aware and attuned to the emotional needs of others.

A chapter is not quite long enough to fully capture the healing process from being broken to being brilliant but hopefully this has given you some hope. That being broken isn't necessarily a bad thing, that it is through being broken that we can learn to develop trust, hope, resourcefulness, and character. That we don't have to fear being broken because it is through this process that we discover who we truly are, and our brilliance can begin to shine!

Like the potter with his prized blue bowl your brokenness is being worked into brilliance. Those pieces which you hold in shame will be put together with gold and you will shine. A whole complete person with a the depth of understanding and maturity to become a priceless work of art.

Carolyn Ferrando

Kristin Sullivan

International Best-Selling Author, Mentor, Speaker & Serial Entrepreneur, USA

Survival mode

To my Grandmother Betty, the kindest soul I ever knew. She always smiled and said hello to everyone, even the birds! She welcomed all into her home and genuinely loved her family more than life itself. She had a heart as big as the Universe, I am so grateful to have had her as a role model.

"Wedding Planning Marries Wellness" – Kristin Sullivan

I inherited my grandmother's gift of intuition, the ability to pay very close attention to those feelings that hit you like a brick dropping in your gut: the warm itchy sweat beading up in the palms of your hands or the solid lump forming in your throat that almost takes your breath away. When you just know that something is off and trying to push you out of your comfort zone, or what I now know as a shift in my alignment. I contribute much of my success as a wedding planner to that very same gift. A gift that has always allowed me time to prepare, to switch gears into what I refer to as "survival mode" or plan B! I am personally a dog lover, however very much like a cat, I always land on my feet. I have lived nine lives pre the age of the big five-oh.

I left high school in the eleventh grade because I thought I was bored; I have learned since then that I had ADD. I could never focus on just one thing; my mind was always racing off in another direction or three. I was street smart with good grades, I was one of the most popular kids, friends with all walks of life but I was lost, so I quit.

I instead worked two jobs while getting my GED. I remained connected with all my friends, some of which are still my very best friends today. Years later I even went on to college to follow, it was there I finally found a focus and passion for business, but I quit there too! With just two classes left I was presented with an opportunity to buy a local travel business; I had always loved to travel, and this was an opportunity which also had a certification program.

So, in 1997 I bought a travel agency and became a certified travel agent and small business owner. I am not sure that the certification process even exists as a true licence any longer. As luck would have it, just shortly after the agency purchase the travel industry was dealt a swift kick in the ass by the airlines when travel bookings shifted to be internet based. This giant shift forced most smaller shops to eventually close their doors.

It was survival time. I had just invested all I had to get deeply involved in my local community. I was the youngest person ever to sit on the local Board of Directors for the Chamber of Commerce, I was one of the only ladies in the local Rotary chapter, and I won Female Young Careerist. I had big plans, therefore I had to think fast and figure out a solution to stay alive. It was then that I decided to turn my passion for gatherings and celebrations into a boutique agency specialising in groups.

During this same time, I was personally struggling with my relationship. I was dating a man 19 years older than me who was a very successful business owner: our age gap and where we were at in business didn't align. We struggled for many years and thought getting married would fix things. In January of 2001 we wed on Little Palm Island in the Florida Keys, it was a nightmare! This will resurface later in my nine lives and is the key reason why I became a wedding planner.

The agency downturn continued to be a big stress point in my marriage with the industry taking such a hit, even though I had married a man of great wealth I took a full-time position as Global Travel & Events Manager for another locally based business, traveling worldwide. I held this position on September 11, 2001. We were headquartered in New Hampshire with offices outside of Boston, our travelers used Boston and Portland airports on a daily basis.

It is a day I, like most, will never forget. I slept on my office floor that night as we manually went through our previous months of paper computer printouts to track each possible traveler.

Our travel computer system was American Express and had gone down, we had no way to easily track people. I was then asked to fly within a week to attempt to curb fear of traveling in support of the company culture. I recall vomiting in the airport bathroom that morning and boarding a nearly empty flight where I sat in complete silence from Boston to Little Rock and back. I left that position shortly after and expanded the travel agency to include destination management services inbound to New England.

In 2004 I got divorced and sold the agency and moved to Key West. In addition to destination weddings, I began traveling for destination sporting events and overseeing luxury events in the automotive space while living bi-coastal for a few years between San Diego and Key West to escape the madness, we call it getting off the rock.

When I finally landed back in Florida full-time after several roller coaster relationships, I met someone that I thought was "the one". He was in law enforcement and appeared safe and honest unlike the last few. To most we looked on the outside like we were living a fairytale life. We resided full-time on a private island with no rent or mortgage, no utility costs or maintenance costs. We took a boat to and from work each day, allowing us to catch both the sunrise and the sunset. We shared a private beach and a dock, he had two of his own boats, we traveled, and we'd recently paid cash for a waterfront lot in the Bahamas to build a second home on. The home was under design while we were awaiting a long, painful and drawn out international legal and permitting process. Thankfully, this delay also caused a delay in the beginning of any construction.

While on a fishing trip in the Florida Keys with friends we got news that we were unable to secure the funding for the build, and found out it is very difficult to get lending for property located outside of the U.S. We had just finalized the home design plans and had cleared the lot. I thought I could figure out a way to make it all come together and exhausted all options. Ultimately, he held this against me, and it turned into anger and non-support of what I wanted to do in business.

He was resentful, distant, and shut down. I suspected for months he was having an affair with someone he worked with, which later would be confirmed. When I look back now, I realize that not only was this another intuitive sign but also blessing in disguise. One month later Hurricane Dorian, the strongest hurricane to ever make landfall sat stalled over the Bahamas for hours upon hours destroying the island. Many lives were lost, and dreams were shattered and washed away during that deadly storm. The land was put up for sale and would be the only reason we really communicated to follow.

I sank into a pretty dark space after things ended between us. This would be the fourth time in my life that I have run from a relationship: two engagements and two marriages to be exact. This I know today stems from deeper trauma in my life having never met my real Father. I know who he is and reached out a few years back. I attempted to connect, and he never followed through. He never married my mother as they were too young. He is married to another woman and, ironically, they named their daughter the same first name as me.

I looked at my maternal Grandfather like my real Father. Later in life I learned he had an affair while married to my grandmother, which devastated me. My Mother had married a man who adopted me when I was young, but he also had an affair and then turned into a dead-beat Dad, never paying support and having other children and additional marriages. So, you can see there is a hurtful pattern here with men.

I have been in and out of therapy for years, I did think the last one was going to work, he had more baggage than I did with three failed marriages. I know we cross paths with people for a reason in life, someday I will know what this path taught me. After we broke up, I learned he had a child he never told me about. Just when you think you know someone, you really do not!

With all that said, I picked myself up, dusted myself off and thought I had finally figured it all out.

Things were turning around and seemed to be falling perfectly into place for 2020. I found a home on the water that fit my master plan. I knew it needed a bit of love, but I was just excited to have a place of my own, with the ability to build out an Airbnb unit and set my business plans into motion.

It was literally like the Candyland game for me: I closed on the house, hired a contractor to gut the downstairs space, I bought a vintage camper to set up as my onsite mobile office, and it even matched my business vision-branding board! I had set a deadline to be up and running by April 1st, I wanted it to be a well-oiled machine prior to my departure for my destination retreats launching in June.

The construction revealed a bit more than expected which is really expected in any renovation project, but I kept forging ahead, all while watching my savings account dwindle.

As someone who has traveled most of her career, I knew what was important as a guest. I spent months staying in Airbnb's, researching and documenting in preparation for this. It was finally time to get it listed and start paying down that mortgage, all part of my business plan. I had finished the package details for what I named "planning-moons". I had scheduled a photo shoot; the staging and decorating was perfectly done down to every last detail.

I was so proud of the design and re-use of space. It made me happy to go sit down there and envision brides and grooms escaping to come sit and relax on their private deck overlooking the water, watching for manatees, dolphins, turtles, and the occasional alligator to swim by. Ending their day with a view of the sky on fire above, witnessing breathtaking sunset views after a day of planning their wedding in a calm and stress-free setting.

I am not one to watch the news each morning as I feel like it just starts my day off hearing only the bad things happening around the world.

I had made it my mission in 2020 to start each day with a positive routine of meditation, yoga, journaling, drinking Rev (a clean energy drink), taking my Usana supplements and diving into my online advanced business education program.

I turned the computer on, logged in and felt one of those strange feelings come over me, something was not right. I began to scan social media and for the first time read the word CoronaVirus. I recall sitting there and saying "well I do not recall the last time I drank a Corona so I should be just fine". Then for a fleeting moment I checked my stock account as I had purchased Anheuser-Busch stock and recalled reading, they owned the Corona Producer. I thought oh great a stock tank!

Boy, do I wish that were the case, as we all know it was not. As I learned more, that survival instinct started to kick in, I focused on all the weddings and events over the next 30 days and what I would do to protect that client experience. What I could not have imagined at that time was looking over the next three hundred days and how my master plan for everything was about to implode. No opening of the Airbnb, no planning-moons, no traveling for retreats and no new wedding planning clients. Just refunds, cancellations and a lack of sleep thinking, how this can be happening!

I fell off the morning health routine fast to instead become plastered in front of the television in pyjamas all hours of the day, watching the world collapse around me. I listened to a business analyst talk about filing for a mortgage forbearance and I did so immediately. I did the same with my mobile office and my vehicle. I applied for PPP and waited.

As a small business owner, we are the ones who got hit the hardest, we all fell between the government cracks of zero help for main street. I was denied. Denied while other companies received in some cases multiple loans with fraudulent documentation.

They say bad news comes in threes. Well, that same week would kickoff the rainy season in Florida, and that is when the shit really started to hit the fan.

My brand new beautiful rental unit began to leak, the cute little white beadboard ceiling was ruined, the rain kept coming and the leaks appeared in multiple places throughout the house. I matched a tear for every raindrop that dripped. I thought I had done everything right, I had every inspection done before buying the house, I relied on the professionals to do what they do.

Sadly, I ended up with a lemon, a lemon of a house, a lemon of an inspection company and ultimately a lemon of a contractor. Yes, this gets worse. Over the course of the next couple of weeks I wandered around the lemon house in a constant state of shock. The repairs I needed to do were to the tune of over fifty thousand dollars.

My savings were gone after the down payment, the move, and the original renovation project. I had maxed out both credit cards equaling another fifty thousand dollars and I started to panic. I then remembered who I was, and that survival mode kicked in.

I am a Planner, I need a damn plan! I started to think about what would happen if I couldn't rent my unit and I couldn't do my weddings and my retreats? I briefly thought about pivoting (a word I now detest more than the word Corona) to a virtual retreat but the very thought of sitting in front of a camera for hours at a time gave me instant anxiety. I am a behind the scenes girl for a reason, I resisted and tossed that idea right out the window.

I read story after story of colleagues and mentors shutting down their physical offices, selling their homes and some even closing their doors for good. As planners we by nature just do not sit still well, we are constantly thinking and juggling for others, in my case I know it is a hidden child coping mechanism. A way to take the focus off looking at myself and my own journey, so taking that away from me forced me on another path inward which scared the hell out of me.

I tried hard to stay focused on something by keeping up with online training, I honestly do believe this (along with my puppy Abaco) saved my life and I will forever be grateful and thankful for my business coach Lisa Johnson.

I needed real life, zero bullshit guidance from someone who had weathered storm after storm and survived. Lisa gave me the inspiration, the tools, and the kick in the ass I needed to make a plan. It was always my intention to launch a retail line once the retreats were up and running. Well, I had plenty of time on my hands now to start using those sleepless nights to do what I do best, which is to plan and create.

I started with the 9P11 bag (now known as Hip-Betty), an emergency kit, created for planners to use onsite/on their person while working at events. Being a person for years that searched for dresses with deep pockets to hide the necessities, this was a top mission of mine. I, of course already carried a kit, an amazing fully stocked kit, but running all over events with a kit that weighed thirty pounds was a nightmare and stuffing my pockets full of items only resulted in the loss of things.

I lost keys, cash, credit cards and so much more. Thus, the inspiration behind the bag, originally the 911 for emergency and the P for Planners, I changed the name just before launching. It is important to note that all my products, despite financial situations, will make annual donations to various charities.

Next in production, after over 2 decades as a planner is my wedding planning guide + journal. It is simply called "a wedding journal".

For years I witnessed people struggle with where to keep important notes about their wedding details, and now knowing what I know and encourage about daily journaling I wanted to give people a tool they would use and cherish.

A Wedding Journal is something meant to be left out as a coffee table book with a reflection of a couple's story and wedding planning journey. I personally selected the artwork to coincide with a planning timeline.

A portion of the journal profits will go to bringing book fairs to schools in poverty, book fairs were always my favorite days in school.

Lastly, while needing to fill another few sleepless nights, I decided to take a creative mental break by taking a class on how to create your own card deck. I aimed to provide a solution here to those who cannot perhaps afford a wedding planner or simply do not want one. My card packs are a very mini version of my retreat business. These cards advise on how to go about the final 30 days before your wedding.

I am only allowing for great things from here on. My focus now is to help fellow planners all around the world through vision board retreats and mentoring. I want others to know that there are options to create recurring revenue for yourself and still do what you love. I wake up to Etsy sales now for products I have already created and simply have to mail off.

For all of you reading this book today, I say to you:

- keep going, keep pushing yourself past your fears and your comfort zones and do not give up. Fail, get back up and fail again! Each time I failed I learned something and got up stronger than before.

- Love yourself first, take care of you first. Establish a morning routine and do your very best to never compromise your beliefs or give up on your dreams. I am walking, living, breathing proof that dreams come true. I would love to connect with you, come retreat with me to plan and lets bring your visions to life.

And lastly

- pay very close attention to your intuition; be guided by those gut feelings, those awkward moments when your body is resisting and let it lead you.

\#

End

"Get Out Of Your Own Way"
Carrie Green, Female Entrepreneurs Association

Gratefully,

Kristin

Your story is not over

How it all began

Deep inside, I feel a great sense of dread, anxiety and fear as continual waves of self-doubt and self-loathing engulf me. The all too familiar feeling of imposter syndrome creeps in, followed by relentless thoughts that are unkind and unhelpful, words that I would never speak of about another person, words that I only use to describe myself. From an early age, I was taught that I was not good enough, smart enough, skinny enough, likeable enough, 'cool' enough and basically, the message I received, understood, and came to believe was that I just was not enough, and I most likely would never be enough.

My self-perception and view of the world and people were marred by trauma. As a child, I learned and grew to hate myself and earnestly believed that I was defective, unworthy, inadequate in every way, and overall, just a waste of a space, a good for nothing that nothing good would come about from. Unfortunately, the negative messages that I was being taught by an alcoholic mother were reaffirmed by schoolyard bullies. As I grew and developed from childhood into adolescence, I was utterly convinced that I was doomed to walk the world alone, isolated from and ridiculed by others, and that there was no hope for me. I learned to hate myself and I even felt like God could not love or accept me because I was such a lost cause.

I learned early in life to not express how I felt, speak my truth, or share my feelings and opinions. I learned to keep how and what I felt suppressed and buried the grief, indescribable pain, and fear deep inside.

I stopped daring to try to change because of multiple past failures, and the reality of my living situation that echoed the harrowing feelings of hopelessness and doom. I feel into a great depression and developed severe social anxiety.

I was failing miserably at school both socially and academically. I felt unloved, unvaluable and unappreciated by my mother. I felt rejected and abandoned by God. I convinced myself that life was only getting more difficult every year I aged and decided that I had had enough. I tried so hard to fit in, to be liked, to be accepted and all I got was constant rejection and ridicule. I reasoned that I was already living in a hellish state and believed that hell could not be much worse than what I was already experiencing. I felt I just could not keep doing this anymore and that no one would have even noticed if or when I disappeared. I just wanted my pain to end.

Plot Twist

I started writing the goodbye letters and stockpiled on the items I would need to make my pain end indefinitely. I decided that I would depart from this world on December 24th, 2001. I had never been so determined and motivated to follow through with action my entire life. This was the only way out that I could think of. Surprisingly, I was invited to go to my visit some family who lived in Brisbane during the 2001 Christmas holidays. I agreed to go believing that this would be my last chance to experience a holiday.

During the holiday, I was shown unconditional love, kindness, generosity, and acceptance. I was raised in a Catholic household but accepted the invitation to attend a Christmas Eve church service at their local church. As I listened to the sermon, I felt an overwhelming desire to respond to the message, and decided to give my heart to Jesus Christ, and asked Him to be my Lord and Saviour. They say God works in mysterious ways, and this rings true on my own life – on the day I had planned to end my life, I became 'born again; and inherited eternal life.

As I read my Bible, I noticed that my beliefs and perceptions of myself, others, and the world, had been marred and distorted through a lens of trauma. I resolved to start loving myself and loving others because God first loved me.

The reason I have chosen to share my beginning with you is to illustrate that, a challenging beginning does not necessarily mean that you will also have a painful ending. If our lives were a story, there is a high probability that there may be many chapters that we wish were not a part of our story, and that there may be many unexpected plot twists along the way.

Whilst we are alive, there is always an opportunity for us to change and develop, but this process of change may not be instantaneous or come easily. It has taken me many years to develop new patterns of thought, develop better/healthier coping mechanisms, learn to love and accept myself (flaws and all), and accept that healing is not a linear process. For me, some days are great, but often, I struggle daily with an inward battle to not live in the past, allow the hurtful words spoken over me to define me, and manage chronic feelings of anxiety and depression.

May I please encourage you to not allow a rocky start to life or a difficult season of your life, to rob you of the unknown possibilities for the future. If you were to tell me as a child that I would be living the life I have now as an adult, I would never have believed you, but none of us can predict that may lie ahead in the future, and for many, what lies ahead is much better than what was before.

Change is Always Possible

Over the years as an adult, I have been re-learning many different truths that counteract and disprove the validity of my self-loathing and self-sabotaging thought, worldview, and behaviours. I have learned firsthand that whilst I am alive, change is always possible, but not necessarily easy. I must admit, I am not naturally the most patient person who you will ever meet, but I am gradually adapting and changing! It can be difficult to accept that change is possible, but not always easy whilst living in a 'microwave' society.

Change as a process is inevitable, try as we may to deny or resist it, change in some form is constantly taking place both within us and around us, each day of our lives. Perhaps you can relate to me and feel that life may have dealt you a hand of 'unwanted' cards, and whilst we sometimes have no control over what cards we are dealt with, we do have control over how we choose to manage the deck of undesired cards we have been dealt.

Have you heard of the saying that a "cheetah cannot change its spots"? This may be true for the cheetah, but the hopeful thing for us as human beings is that we can and are able to change! Change in and of itself is a process, which can either have positive or negative impacts on and in our lives. We may not be able to control the processes of change around us, but we can learn to manage other changes in our lives such as how we react to circumstances, and our behaviours.

For example, I cannot control when someone speaks harshly of or to me, but I can choose whether I will allow what has been said, to define me or refine me. When unkind words penetrate through to my heart, and my mind starts re-telling the story I believed for so long as a child (I am not good enough, no one likes me, I am worthless, etc), I am learning to be aware of these thoughts, acknowledge why I feel this way and then reframe my thinking to something like "those words are not an accurate reflection of me, rather they are a reflection of where that person is at the moment", and then I employ the use of curiosity by pondering what has happened or is going on in that person's life that is making them act in such a way.

Your story matters

One of the fundamental beliefs I have as a counsellor is that every person has a story, and every story matters. One of the greatest concerns I have and something that I have become acutely aware of, is that so many of us have our feelings, experiences and opinions invalidated multiple times a day. What are thoughts on this? I wonder how many of you may agree or disagree with what I have said?

Although, I do not think that everyone intentionally seeks out to invalidate others', sometimes a lack of self-awareness may result in invalidating others' experiences and feelings. For example, have you ever experienced when you have shared something personal with another person, who seem to be more interested in responding rather than listening, and retorts by telling you how their experience was more significant? For example, have you ever heard something along the lines of: "Oh really? You're so lucky! When I had my operation, I had to stay in hospital for _____ number of nights afterwards because my surgery must have been more serious than yours"; "You think you have it bad, I had it so much worse!"; "You'll get over it – I went through the same thing"; or "It's really not that much of a big deal, wait until you hear what happened to me!".

Have you ever experienced a similar response like those listed above? If so, how did it make you feel? I am going to guess that hearing a response that downplayed or invalidated your experience or feelings, probably made you feel insignificant in comparison, or maybe you even felt a bit embarrassed or awkward for sharing when someone else 'had it worse'. All too often, our stories can become interpreted as being less important or inspirational when compared to another person's story. May I please encourage you to embrace your story (the not so glamourous parts and all), be proud of your story and share your story if you feel safe and ready to do so? It does not matter if your story is different to others because each one of us has unique experiences and interpretation of these experiences, and that is okay. In fact, that is a beautiful thing!

Try to not fall into the trap of comparing your story with someone else's, because your story matters because you matter, and you do not have to justify any difference between your experience and someone else's experience. Just because someone's experience is different to your own – it does not make their experience more significant, better, or more important than your experience, it just means that their story may be a little different to your story and that is perfectly okay.

It may be a learned skill for us to learn how to validate our own story whilst also validating other people's stories, especially if their experiences, feelings, or opinions are different to our own. We may have to learn to adopt a both/and way of thinking to accommodate both our own stories and other's stories simultaneously, but it is possible to do so.

Your Greatest Strength and Your Greatest Weakness

Perhaps you can relate to some of the things I have shared about my childhood or my life? As mentioned earlier, I think each one of us may have a few chapters in our life story that we are not so proud of, or perhaps may even be ashamed of? Personally, I do not like talking about my biological mother as every time she is brought up, a flood of traumatic memories arises within me. Whilst I can recognise and acknowledge the origins of these traumatic responses, I prefer not to focus on them consistently.

What I perceived as my greatest weakness, has also turned up to be my greatest strength. I honestly do not think that I would be as effective as a counsellor if I had not experienced certain circumstances in my life. From my brokenness, came a deep sense of compassion for others and a desire for justice. The painful and traumatic experiences from my past have had both a negative and a positive effect on me, and so can be the same of anyone else. Just because we have been hurt by others does not give us the right to hurt others.

Each one of us has the tremendous power to either hurt or heal, build up or tear down, or help or hinder. Carl Jung famously stated, "what we resist persists", and this rings true when we try to deny or suppress the parts of our past that we are unfond, ashamed or fearful of. We can recognise and acknowledge how the past may have shaped and influenced us, but if are unhappy with how we are living in the present – change is always possible, but not necessarily easy!

Be kind to yourselves and each other during this journey we are all embarking on called life. Remember that each of us has a story, and each of our stories matter because each of us matter! Cheetahs may not be able to change their spots, but you can if you would like to do so. Change is always a possibility, but it may not happen instantaneously or effortlessly. Each of you possess an incredible ability to be agents of positive change in your personal, professional, and social lives! Never forget that each of you have the capacity to be inspirational and live inspiring lives. Finally, never forget that just because you may have had a rocky start to life, or are going through a tough season of life, this does not necessarily mean that the ending to your story will not be inspirational – because your story is not over yet.

Thank you for reading this, I hope it resonates,

Tam

Authors Biographies

Christine Innes is a Coach, Speaker, #1 International Best Seller Author, host of The Corporate Escapists Podcast, and editor-in-chief of The Corporate Escapists Magazine.

Christine is the CEO and Founder of The Corporate Escapists, a global company empowering people to transform their lives by letting go of their corporate identity and finding and following their passion.

Christine's clients say:

" I have been lucky to be featured in the magazine, however, what I cherished the most is that Christine has held my hand through the process of rebranding. I love it! I highly recommend anyone wishing to have a fabulous take in a new direction to call Christine, she is a champion through and through." - Dr. Anne-Marie

"Christine has been our business coach at Curious Me for several months. Wow, what a difference one-on-one coaching makes! Christine gave us the inspiration, motivation, and accountability we needed to go from planning for the now, to see the future. We started setting ourselves serious business goals and with her help, put in place action plans and timelines to make it happen. We experienced our best financial quarter EVER, even with COVID interruptions. all thanks to her help. We are forever grateful for Christine, her support, mentorship, and friendship." - Curious Me

Christine is passionate about helping people be themselves and create a life they love.

Christine offers 1:1 coaching with her two signature programs:

EmpowHER: A 12-week program helping you go from corporate mess to your empowHERed best

The Corporate Kickoff Program: A 60-day program to launch your business online.

Connect with Christine here:
Facebook; @christineinnescoach @thecorporateescapists
Instagram: @christine_innes @thecorporateescapists
Website: www.thecorporateescapists.com

Kleo Merrick is an International Bestselling Author, Speaker, Online Business Strategist.

Kleo is the CEO of Merrick Courses, a company she founded in 2013 where she runs successful Workshops, Online Training Programs and teaches businesses how to package their services by creating Online Courses and how to manoeuvre Digital Marketing for Entrepreneurs.

Her clients say: "Kleo taught me more in 2 hours than it would have taken me 5 years to learn myself...!!!" – Cathy Kingsley

She is the author of, 'I Did It: 16 Mindset Secrets To Transform The Life You Have Into The Ultimate Life you Desire', 'Yes I Can: 16 Success Secrets Form Inspiring Women Around The World' and 'Compelling Selling: How To Earn More By Selling Less' and creator of her following signature programs:

'Entrepreneurs Academy' - Online Business School focused on supporting Small Business Owners with Entrepreneurial Business Skills.

'Online Course Academy' – 6-week Online Program How to Create & Sell your 1st Online Course.

'Accelerated Webinar Program' – 6-week Online Program to Simply and Easily create Webinars from scratch, without any of the Techy Jargon.

'Online Course Mastery Program' – 12 Month Mentoring Program to Convert your current Knowledge into Tangible, Saleable & Irresistible Online Content on Autopilot.

Kleo is extremely passionate about Creating a Community of Passionate Business Owners and Upskilling them to the Digital World.

Merrick Courses Pty Ltd
www.kleomerrick.com
kleo@kleomerrick.com
Facebook: https://www.facebook.com/kleomerrickpage/
Instagram: https://www.instagram.com/kleomerrick/
LinkedIn: https://www.linkedin.com/in/kleomerrick/

Justine is a Rehabilitation Counsellor and Coach who spent the first 23 years of her life in New Zealand where she learnt the art of entertaining others and building a solid Kiwi identity.

She currently lives in Brisbane, Australia with her husband of 16 years and their daughter, Astrid.

Justine is a first time author who has always loved to write and admits to owning many journals that are filled with her musings. She has always used writing to help her through the hard times and is excited to achieve her dream of being published.

Justine has recently launched her counselling and coaching business where she helps professionals get unstuck and achieve their goals. She is also the founder of Job Searching Mums, a service dedicated to helping Mums make a successful return to the workforce.

Online courses

'6 steps to future proof yourself' - 6 week course designed for those who are just starting their personal development journey.

'12 ways to experience personal growth' - 12 week course designed to further your personal development journey.

For further information on these courses, please email Justine via the address below:

RC Counselling and Coaching
www.rccounsellingandcoaching.com.au
justine@rccounsellingandcoaching.com.au
Facebook: https://www.facebook.com/rccounsellingandcoaching
Instagram: https://www.instagram.com/rccounsellingandcoaching

Job Searching Mums
Facebook: https://www.facebook.com/jobsearchingmums
Instagram: https://www.instagram.com/jobsearchingmums

LinkedIn: https://www.linkedin.com/in/justine-lawson-576132208

Currently based in Sydney and with clients worldwide, Ana Angelique is a wellbeing life coach, mentor, author and public speaker, who's had her thought-provoking articles on being authentic and living your best life, published in various magazines. Her teachings are geared towards working mothers, who are seeking balance, harmony, happiness and fulfilment in their lives.

Ana's positive approach to life, her captivating and addictive energy, and her creative thinking, enable her to empower her clients to take charge of their future and regain control. She has an insider's perspective - one that's been gained from an international corporate background and being a mother, and it enables her to relate to and understand, the real challenges faced by women every day.

Ana believes that others shouldn't have to struggle in silence like she did, overcoming major life challenges in isolation, because as complex as life can be, it's also beautiful and should be enjoyed; And she believes that you can have it all.

Inspirational and persuasive, Ana is a thought leader and change advocate who has natural teaching abilities and is known for her unique perspective on situations.

Your True North
www.your-true-north.com.au
ana.angelique.guide@gmail.com
Facebook: https://www.facebook.com/ana.angelique.guide
Instagram: https://www.instagram.com/yourtruenorth_au/
LinkedIn: https://www.linkedin.com/in/wellbeing-life-coach/

Kylie James is an Executive Coach, People Strategist, Champion of Change, and Author.

Kylie is the founder of Kylie James Coaching, a business she founded in 2021 empowering people to live their best life by discovering how they can become more visible in their own world.

She combines her leadership, coaching and Human Resources (HR) expertise to create and deliver practical, people focussed solutions so:

- **Individuals** can find a good rhythm with their work and home life without feeling overwhelmed and burnt out
- **Teams** can have clarity on their role so they can deliver great outcomes to their leaders, stakeholders and clients
- **Leaders and Managers** can understand and communicate what success looks like so their team is seen as trusted advisors and high performers
- **HR practitioners** can support their people and organisation.

Her clients say:

"Kylie keeps me grounded and reminds me of what I can control. I leave our chats feeling inspired. I have more perspective and am ready to tackle the world" – Casey

Kylie James Coaching
www.kyliejames.com.au
kylie@kyliejames.com.au
Facebook: https://www.facebook.com/kyliejamescoaching
Instagram: https://www.instagram.com/kyliejamescoaching
LinkedIn: www.linkedin.com/in/kylie-james-cphr-6a066b20

Lisa Ohtaras is a renowned Energy Healer, Soul Healer, Intuitive Spiritual Coach, Spiritual Educator, Reiki Master, Seichim Master, Medium, Channel & Soulful Forgiveness Workshop Facilitator.

Over two decades ago, Lisa healed herself of Multiple Sclerosis (M.S.) warning signs. Her diagnosis initiated an awakening from her spiritual slumber and connected Lisa to her inner self.

Lisa transformed pain, numbness alternating with pins and needles in her hands and arms, feet and legs, night sweats, insomnia, chronic fatigue and visual challenges, all without medication.

Through her Spiritual connection, consistent daily meditation, personal growth, Spiritual growth and development, Lisa restored balance, harmony and well-being to her physical body and emotional state.

Following Lisa's self-healing, she continued working in her nursing career which collectively spanned over two decades. Then in 2003, Lisa commenced living her Soul Purpose and Sacred Contract and has been helping people with physical and life challenges, emotional matters of the heart and forgiveness challenges, to live in balance, harmony, health and the greatest version of themselves.

Caring Energetic Healing
www.caringenergetichealing.com
Lisa@caringenergetichealing.com
Facebook: https://www.facebook.com/lisaohtaras
Instagram: https://www.instagram.com/lisaohtaras
Linkedin: https://www.linkedin.com/in/lisaohtaras

Terri is an International Best-Selling author; ghostwriter, speaker; facilitator; mentor and coach.

She is the face of Connect Within, and is based in the northern suburbs of Brisbane. Her clients are heard, validated, acknowledged, encouraged and supported to find the solutions they are searching for.

Terri believes every person has the capacity within them to create the life they choose to have, and to write and share their story. By assisting her clients to transition and transform, a ripple effect is created when they are able to empower others by paying it forward.

Terri aspires to inspire the people she meets to reach their potential, as inspiration leads to motivation, and motivation leads to action, providing results.

Her life has been a journey of ups and downs, trials and tribulations, both personally and professionally.

She is a life-long learner, seeks out new opportunities, is an avid writer and reader and loves to travel.

Terri draws on her diverse skills developed through her experiences, numerous employment opportunities, networking, and cultural awareness from the many locations in which she has lived.

If you want to reclaim your zest for life and your motivation to live your life by design, rather than by default, Terri will work with you to achieve your goals.

Happiness is a choice, and you can choose it every day.

Connect Within
www.connectwithin.com.au
terri@connectwithin.com.au
Facebook: https://www.facebook.com/connectwithinmindsetlifecoach/
LinkedIn: https://www.linkedin.com/in/terri-tonkin/

Carolyn Ferrando is one half of the creative agency Hawthorne Creative.

Together with her brother-in-law and business partner Alex, they provide digital marketing, photography and videography services for individuals and businesses across South East Queensland.

Undoubtably, Carolyn's passion is people, and she daily looks for ways to meaningfully connect with others to actively bring joy to their lives.

Hawthorne Creative
www.hawthornecreative.com.au
info@hawthornecreative.com.au
Facebook, Instagram, LinkedIn & YouTube @hawthornecreativemedia
LinkedIn : @CarolynMareeFerrando

After two decades they call her, "Chief Celebration Officer".

Kristin Sullivan of Swivel Group Events is known for executing destination celebrations to remember, designing unforgettable weddings, milestone birthdays, anniversaries and corporate VIP experiences for thousands of couples and corporate clients. Kristin has expanded into the world of wellness, marrying it to wedding planning by creating The Bridal Retreat, a holistic space for the newly engaged to retreat to plan.

Kristin is the North America Mentor for The Global Wedding Academy, the weekly host of the "Just As Planned" a Wedding Planning Podcast Series. She is an International Best-Selling Author who has been quoted on People.com, and featured in several magazines with one of her weddings featured on ABC Primetime.

She spent the 2020 pandemic designing, creating and producing her retail line to include a planner emergency tool bag, a set of wedding planning + wellness cards and a wedding journal & guide. Kristin also became a Dare to Declare Certified Vision Board Instructor. Kristin loves spending time with her dog Abaco and is passionate about traveling.

The Bridal Retreat & Swivel Group Events
www.thebridalretreat.com
www.swivelgroupevents.com
kristin@thebridalretreat.com
Campsite: @thebridalretreat - Campsite
Facebook: https://www.facebook.com/shecomesfromboston
Pinterest:https://pin.it/6iZRcGE
Instagram: @thebridalretreat
LinkedIn: https://www.linkedin.com/in/kristin-sullivan-a770551a5
Twitter: https://twitter.com/retreat_bridal
YouTube: leftovercakechat - YouTube
Podcast: Let's talk weddings - YouTube

Kristin Sullivan

Tamara Hall is a counsellor and the founder of Strong Mind Healthy Body.

She graduated with a Bachelor of Applied Social Science from the Australian College of Applied Psychology in 2013, and has worked in a multitude of different workplaces, including in private practice.

She is currently studying a double Master's degree in Social Work and Mental Health Practice, and is passionate about mental health and social justice.

She is a wife, fur baby mama and a lover of poetry and jigsaw puzzles.

If you would like to connect with Tamara, please feel free to do so by touching base on her Instagram account @strongmindhealthybody